Canadian Arctic Prehistory

Canadian Prehistory Series

A growing interest in Canadian prehistory and the introduction of new archaeological techniques have resulted in significant discoveries across Canada. This series enables the general reader to enjoy for the first time a popular account of these exciting new findings in Canadian prehistory. Each book explores the prehistory of a particular geographical or cultural area and the authors, who are leading scholars in their fields, describe many fascinating aspects of archaeological research. Time charts, graphs, maps, and numerous photographs and drawings recreate a vivid picture of the life of the native peoples in Canada before Jacques Cartier.

Canadian Arctic Prehistory

Robert McGhee

Canadian Museum of Civilization

CANADIAN CATALOGUING IN PUBLICATION DATA

McGhee, Robert, 1941–
    Canadian arctic prehistory

(Canadian prehistory series)

ISBN 0-660-02477-2

1. Eskimos – Canada – Antiquities. 2. Canada, Northern – Antiquities.
3. Arctic regions – Antiquities. I. Title. II. Series.

E99.E7M312   970'.004'97   C77-001777-0

Design: Brant Cowie/Artplus Ltd.

Cover: This ivory carving of a polar bear carries marks representing
the skeleton and joints; a slit beneath the throat contains a sliver of
ivory. The marks on the carving are probably of magical significance,
and the bear may represent the spirit-helper of a shaman. The carving
was found in a Dorset site near Igloolik.

Contents

List of Illustrations

Colour Plates

Black-and-White Plates

Maps

Diagrams

Introduction

There was once a world before this, and in it lived people who were not of our tribe. But the pillars of the earth collapsed, and all were destroyed. And the world was emptiness. Then two men grew up from a hummock of earth. They were born and fully grown all at once. And they wished to have children. A magic song changed one of them into a woman, and they had children. These were our earliest forefathers, and from them all the lands were peopled.
Tuglik, Igloolik area, 1922

Thus, Inuit mythology tells of the creation of the earth and of mankind. After the creation came a mythical age, similar to the "once-upon-a-time" of European storytellers, when the world was inhabited by strange races of giants and dwarfs, and men could turn into animals or spirits. During this age, the sun evolved from a girl who fled to the sky, chased by her incestuous brother, who was to become the moon. The mammals of the sea grew from the fingers of a girl who was thrown out of a boat during a storm. Her father chopped off her fingers as she clung to the boat, and she sank to the bottom of the sea to become the most powerful spirit of all, the ruler of the sea beasts. During this mythical age, the various races of mankind originated from a girl who married a dog and set her more-or-less-human offspring adrift in a boot to populate the world with Inuit, Indian and European peoples. Legends that apparently relate to a more recent time tell of the Tunit, a gentle race that occupied arctic Canada when the ancestors of the Inuit arrived in the area. The legends of the distant past fade gradually into stories of events that occurred only a few generations ago, or within the memories of living people.

1

These myths and legends provided a historical environment for the Inuit, enriching the physical world by peopling it with figures and events from the magical past. Inuit mythology, like that of the Europeans, also served to explain aspects of the present world in terms of past events. The aims of this book are the same as those of the traditional storyteller: to explain the present arctic world by telling of events that happened in the distant past.

The prehistorian approaches the past on a different level than the storyteller, however, in that he asks specific questions that are only vaguely dealt with in mythology. Where did the Inuit come from, and how are they related to other races? When did they arrive in arctic North America, and what brought them to a land so cold and barren that no other people has found it habitable? How, with such a tiny population, did they establish and maintain mastery over approximately one-fiftieth of the land area of earth?

To answer these questions we must turn to archaeology, to the study of the remains of villages and camps occupied by the ancestors of the Inuit. By excavating and studying these remains we can obtain a vague idea of the way of life led by the people who lived there in the distant past. The traces of houses or tent foundations can tell us the approximate size of the settlements. The bones of the animals that were used as food are preserved in the frozen arctic soil, indicating what the people lived on. These same bones, as well as the charcoal from cooking fires, can be analyzed by the radiocarbon dating method to determine the approximate age of the site. Tools and weapons that were lost or discarded by the inhabitants can be compared with those recovered from other excavations to discover how technology has changed over time.

The picture of arctic prehistory that emerges from such a study is necessarily vague and uncertain. Because this book omits many of the details and arguments of interest only to the professional archaeologist, readers may get the impression that arctic prehistory is straightforward and well understood. They should realize that our present picture is based on the excavation of a very small sample of prehistoric sites, and is therefore almost certainly biased by the chance nature of archaeological findings. We may be sure that a few more years of archaeological work will produce changes in the outline presented in this book, and will fill in many of the details that are now obscure.

Readers may be confused by the use of the terms *Inuit* and *Eskimo*. The Eskimo peoples of arctic Canada, as well as those of North Alaska and Greenland, speak dialects of a single Eskimo language, *inuktitut*, in which they refer to themselves as *inuit*. This is the name they prefer to be known by, and the term is useful to the prehistorian who wishes to distinguish them from other Eskimo peoples. The Eskimo populations of West Alaska, South Alaska, and Siberia speak other related Eskimo languages and do not think of themselves as *inuit*. In this book the term *Eskimo* includes all peoples that speak languages of the Eskimo type, and ancient peoples whose archaeological remains indicate that they were of the "Eskimo tradition" but whose languages are not known. *Inuit* is used to refer to the present occupants of the area between Bering Strait and Greenland, and to their archaeological ancestors of about the past thousand years.

CHAPTER 1

The First Arctic Explorers

Palaeolithic Indians (30 000–5000 B.C.)

Primitive country, rock chiefly,
Destitute of wood,
Gravelly hills and marshy meadows,
Frequented by large herds of Reindeer,
Ranges of hills on both sides of the river, round backed
  and barren,
Killed Musk Oxen here.
Notations from Sir John Franklin's map of the Barren Grounds, 1820–21

The ice sheets of the last glaciation covered most of arctic Canada between about 30 000 and 15 000 years ago. Only the western portion of Banks Island and the region around the Mackenzie Delta remained unglaciated, the eastern edge of a large unglaciated area that stretched across the northern Yukon, Alaska and eastern Siberia. With much of the earth's water locked up in continental glaciers, sea levels dropped to expose the shallow bottom of the Bering Sea, thus creating a land bridge about a thousand kilometres wide joining Siberia to Alaska. Across the land bridge came the first human occupants of North America: Palaeolithic Siberian hunters of the caribou, mammoth and other large animals that grazed on the Ice Age tundras. By approximately 30 000 years ago these hunters may have reached the northern Yukon, where objects which have been identified as possible tools have been found in river deposits of the Old Crow Flats area. Perhaps at this time, or later, some of these people moved southwards to become the ancestors of the American Indians.

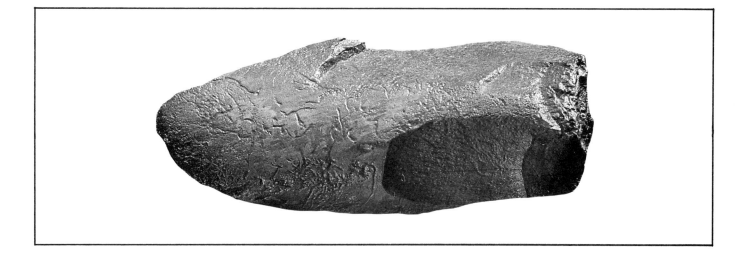

Plate 1. A Possible 30 000-Year-Old Artifact from the Yukon
Tonnes of fossilized animal bones have been recovered from the gravel bars of rivers in the Old Crow Flats area. A few of these bones may have been split or flaked to be used as tools. This sharp-edged flake of bone has been removed from the leg bone of a mammoth, by a heavy blow struck while the bone was still fresh. It has been radiocarbon dated to around 30 000 years ago.

About 15 000 years ago the glaciers began to melt and retreat. By about 10 000 years ago the entire western Arctic had been deglaciated, and the waters of the Bering Sea had risen to drown the land bridge, thereby separating Alaska and Siberia. The ice sheets continued to melt as the climate became warmer, and just under 7000 years ago they had retreated to the mountains of the eastern Arctic, where they still remain as small glaciers. From beneath the ice emerged the landscape of arctic Canada, great silent plains of rock and gravel with no trace of vegetation and no animal life.

The first living forms arrived by sea. The remains of shellfish and the bones of whales are found on beaches formed more than 9000 years ago along the channels of the arctic archipelago. Driftwood began to appear on the beaches as forests became established in the valleys of the Mackenzie River and the great northward-flowing rivers of Siberia. The whale bones and driftwood indicate that the arctic seas were not permanently frozen at this time, and there are some hints that between 8000 and 4000 years ago there was much less sea ice than at present. The open waters of the postglacial arctic seas

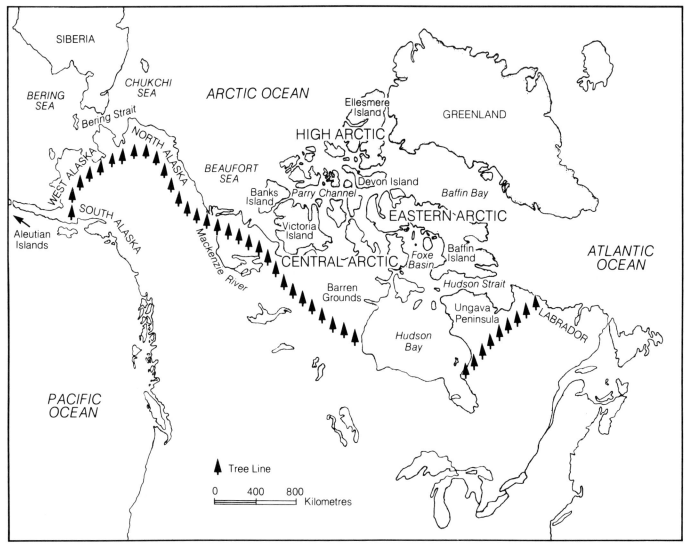

Map 1. Arctic North America

Map 2. The Northern World in the Last Ice Age About the middle of the last Ice Age, the northern world may have looked something like this. To the south of the glaciers were large areas of tundra populated by caribou, mammoth, bison, horses, and other large animals. These animals were hunted by Old-World Upper Palaeolithic people, some of whom crossed the Bering land bridge and passed through arctic North America to become the ancestors of the American Indians. The only traces of their passage are bone tools found in the Old Crow Flats area of the Northern Yukon, which have been dated to about 30 000 years ago.

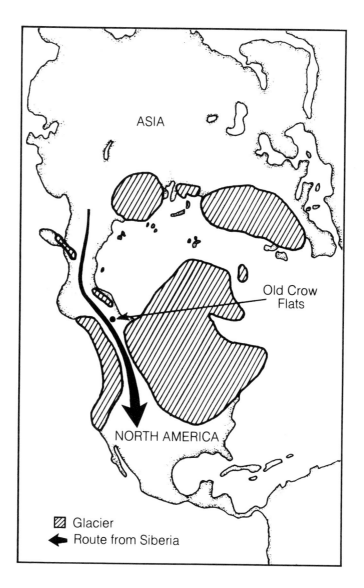

ASIA

Old Crow Flats

NORTH AMERICA

🗘 Glacier
← Route from Siberia

must have been quickly populated by a wide range of sea mammals, fish and birds.

At about the same time, vegetation was gradually becoming established on the arctic mainland and islands as the seeds and spores of flowering plants and lichens were carried northwards by wind, running water, and migrating birds. The climate of arctic Canada during the early postglacial period was somewhat warmer than at present, and tundra vegetation similar to today's probably became established in most areas within a few centuries of deglaciation. Between 8000 and 4000 years ago the tree line, that is, the northern edge of the coniferous forest, was considerably farther north than it is today. Land animals, including the migratory caribou, moved northwards as well, and were soon followed by the first human hunters to occupy arctic Canada.

These first immigrants to the Canadian Arctic were Indians, the descendants of people who had developed a big-game-hunting way of life in the mid-latitude tundra areas south of the continental glaciers. As early as 9000 years ago, an eastern branch of these Indians had moved north of the Gulf of St. Lawrence and reached the Strait of Belle Isle region of southern Labrador. Here they hunted caribou and developed techniques for exploiting the rich sea-mammal resources of the area. By 4500 years ago, these Indians had occupied Labrador as far north as Saglek Bay, only 200 kilometres south of Hudson Strait. Although the Maritime Archaic Indians successfully adapted to the subarctic coastal environment of Labrador, we do not think that they ever moved into the true arctic regions of Hudson Strait or Baffin Island. They were displaced from coastal Labrador about 2000 years ago, but their relatives survived in the Atlantic Provinces and were probably ances-

Map 3. Early Occupations of Arctic North America   In the early post-glacial period, between 12 000 and 7000 years ago, the glaciers retreated rapidly and the northern climate became warmer. Northern North America attracted Siberian populations, who crossed the shrinking Bering land bridge (A), as well as American Indian groups. We can trace three northern movements by Indians: one to the Yukon and Alaska that began about 11 000 years ago (B), a second about 9000 years ago along the Atlantic coast (D), and a third to the Barren Grounds at least 8000 years ago (C). The map shows continental glaciers as they were about 8000 years ago.

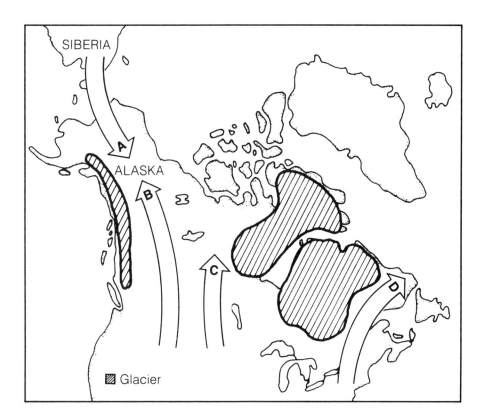

tral to the Eastern Algonkian peoples (Beothuk, Micmac, Malecite) of eastern Canada.

A second northward movement of Indian populations began as early as 8000 years ago in the Barren Grounds, between Hudson Bay and Great Bear Lake. These migrants were caribou hunters, whose technology included spear points of the type used by the early bison hunters of the northern plains area. Some of these groups appear to have adapted their hunting techniques to the pursuit of caribou in the northern forests and southern tundra. Their descendants may have developed the Shield Archaic tradition, a way of life based on inland fishing and northern forest hunting, which is found archaeologically from Keewatin to interior Labrador and dates to the period between 7000 and 3000 years ago. It has been suggested that the Shield Archaic people were ancestral to those Indians of the northern bush who spoke Northern Algonkian languages (Cree, Ojibwa, Naskapi, Montagnais, and others).

To the west of the Mackenzie River, in the mountain passes and forested valleys of the Yukon and Alaska, there is rather confusing archaeological evidence of Indian occupation over a long period of time. This is the route by which the early ancestors of the American Indians must have reached central North America, but as yet we have found no trace of their passage aside from the Old Crow Flats material mentioned earlier. We do find traces of another Indian movement northward, which began about 11 000 years ago, of people who brought with them the distinctive fluted spear points of Plains hunters. In Alaska these people may have met recent immigrants from Siberia, who had crossed the Bering land bridge shortly before it was drowned by rising sea levels about 10 000 years ago. These immigrants brought with them a stone tool industry

Plate 2. Stone Tools Made by Immigrants from Siberia about 10 000 Years Ago The small, parallel-sided slivers of stone at lower right are microblades, which were struck from a microblade core like the one shown at lower left. This specialized and efficient way of making stone tools was used throughout northern Eurasia in the early postglacial period, and appeared in Alaska about 10 000 years ago. The people who brought this technique across the shrinking Bering land bridge may have been ancient ancestors of either the Eskimos or the Athapaskan Indians. Microblades were a basic element of later arctic technologies and were manufactured in arctic Canada until about 1000 years ago. The large stone core and the spear point are from the same Alaska Peninsula site and are radiocarbon-dated slightly later than 10 000 years ago. Photograph by Don E. Dumond.

based on Siberian Mesolithic styles, including the use of microblades—small, sharp-edged slivers of stone made by a specialized technique and used to give sharp cutting edges to bone spears and knives. These users of Siberian microblades were probably the last population to enter North America by land, and many archaeologists suspect that they were the ancestors of the Athapaskan Indians of northwestern Canada and Alaska. Others think that they were ancestral to the Eskimos.

While Indians were establishing themselves throughout the northern forests of Canada, the arctic tundras and the seasonally frozen oceans to the north remained unoccupied. Indians who hunted in the southern tundra appear to have remained fairly close to the tree line, so that they could retreat to the forest during the winter. This was the pattern of life followed during the eighteenth century by the Chipewyan Indians of the Barren Grounds, and a similar pattern seems to have been characteristic of earlier Indian occupations. Evidence from geology, zoology and palaeobotany indicates that by at least 8000 years ago the environment of much of arctic Canada was similar to present conditions, and perhaps was even richer for hunting peoples. Why then did most of this region remain unoccupied until much later?

The answer to this question almost certainly lies in the need for a very specialized technology and way of life to adapt to those tundra regions from which there was no retreat to winter shelter in the forests. Such a technology and adaptation had apparently not been developed at the time the Indians began to occupy northern Canada. For 4000 years after it had become habitable, most of arctic Canada lay unoccupied, while to the west, in Siberia or Alaska, a group of people were developing a way of life that would allow them to exploit the abundant caribou, fish and sea mammals of the arctic zone.

CHAPTER 2

Eskimo Origins

Canada, Alaska or Siberia? (6000–2000 B.C.)

*Our Greenlanders, it should seem, having settled in Tartary
after the grand dispersion of the nations, were gradually
impelled northward by the tide of emigration, till they
reached the extreme corner of Kamtschatka, and finding
themselves disturbed even in these remote seats, they
crossed the Strait to the neighboring continent of America.*
David Crantz, History of Greenland, 1767

The origin of the Eskimos has fascinated European scholars
for the past two centuries. The first to publish a theory on the
subject was David Crantz, an eighteenth-century Moravian
missionary to Greenland. Crantz noted similarities between the
Eskimos and the peoples of "Great Tartary between Mongolia
and the Arctic Ocean," and on this basis suggested that the
Eskimos had recently crossed the Bering Strait from Siberia.
This idea was challenged by nineteenth-century scholars, who
saw similarities between the culture of the Eskimos and that of
the Upper Palaeolithic caribou hunters who occupied Europe
during the closing phases of the last Ice Age; following the re-
treating glaciers northwards and eastwards from Europe, the
ancestors of the Eskimos were supposed to have eventually
crossed the Bering Strait and reached arctic North America.

During the late nineteenth and early twentieth centuries,
some prehistorians began to relate the Eskimo to the American
Indian, suggesting that Eskimo origins lay in subarctic Canada.
The ancient Eskimos were seen as a tribe of Indians that had
moved north of the tree line to the Barren Grounds west of
Hudson Bay. The interior Caribou Eskimos, who occupied the
Barren Grounds during the early twentieth century, were seen
as living relics of this ancient way of life. According to this
scheme, some of the early Eskimos moved northwards to
the arctic coast, where they learned to hunt sea mammals,

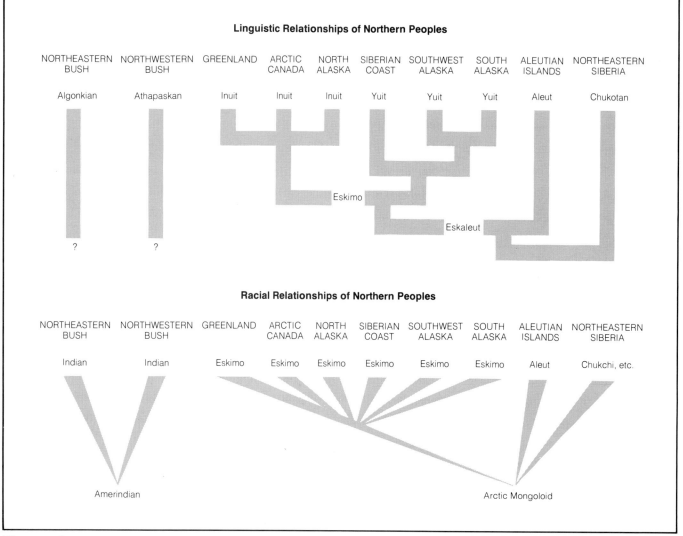

Diagram 1.

and their descendants spread east to Greenland and west to Alaska, where they formed the Eskimo populations of the historic period.

Anthropological and archaeological work of the past fifty years has shown that none of these theories are likely to be correct. The idea of a Central Arctic origin has been ruled out by detailed comparisons showing that the Eskimos are not closely related to American Indians in race, language or culture. Rather, in all these characteristics, the Eskimos are more closely related to the Aleuts of the Aleutian Islands and to peoples of the Chukchi and Kamchatka peninsulas of northeastern Siberia.

The Eskimo and Aleut languages are closely related and almost certainly developed from a single ancient language (called Eskaleut) spoken several thousand years ago. The Eskaleut language is in turn related to the Chukotan languages spoken by the Chukchi, Koryak and Kamchadal peoples of northeastern Siberia. Along with the linguistic relationship, there are relationships in other areas of culture—mythology, religion and technology. Physically, the Eskimos and Aleuts belong to a distinctive racial group known as Arctic Mongoloid. The Chukotan-speaking peoples of northeastern Siberia are also Arctic Mongoloids, but no American Indians are members of this racial group.

Since the peoples most closely related to the Eskimos live around the Bering Sea, this area is the most likely to yield answers to the question of Eskimo origins. The Bering Sea, which was largely dry land until about 10 000 years ago, may have been occupied by the ancestors of American Indians. If this is true, then the ancestors of the Eskimos must have reached the area at some time after 10 000 years ago. We must now turn to a study of the archaeological remains of these ancient Eskimos to resolve these questions.

Although comparative studies tell us roughly where we should look for these remains—along the Bering Sea coasts at some time after 10 000 years ago—they do not tell us what we should look for, or how we can recognize ancient Eskimo sites when we do find them. Accordingly, we now enter a world of "possibles" and "probables" and "maybes," words that still take up a good deal of space in any archaeological history of the Eskimos. Most of these qualifying words are left out of the present account. Four alternative schemes of early Eskimo prehistory are summarized in the accompanying Diagram 2, but our present knowledge is not adequate to indicate which, if any, of the four is correct.

The earliest-known archaeological remains from the coasts of the Bering Sea come from Anangula Island, a small island near the eastern end of the Aleutian chain. The earliest occupation was at the Anangula Blade site, dated between roughly 8500 and 7000 years ago, and is thus close in time as well as place to the sort of archaeological occupation we suspect might be ancestral to the Eskimos or Aleuts or perhaps both. The remains at Anangula consist mostly of chipped-stone tools, almost all of them simple flakes of stone or the more standardized parallel-sided flakes known as blades. Many have been shaped by removing small flakes from one side to form a variety of cutting and scraping tools. The presence of blades and microblades suggests a relationship to peoples of both interior Alaska and Siberia, who were making these stone tools at about the same time, but the specific forms of the artifacts indicate that the relationship was not very close.

The archaeologists who have worked at Anangula suggest that this early occupation represents people who were adapted to exploiting the coastal resources of the North Pacific, and whose ancestors had spread across the southern rim of the Bering land bridge during the closing phases of the last Ice Age. When the land bridge became flooded, some of these people remained in Alaska and continued to follow their maritime adaptation in the Aleutian Islands. The descendants of the people of the Anangula Blade site may have continued to live in the Aleutians until the present time. The Anangula Village site, occupied between roughly 6000 and 4500 years ago, and the Chaluka site on nearby Umnak Island, occupied from 4000 years ago until the last century, may represent the remains of this continuous occupation. If so, then these people were ancestral to the Aleuts who occupied the area during historic times.

If it is true that the Anangula people of 8500 years ago were ancestral Aleuts, this is of great importance in our search for Eskimo origins. The Aleuts are the closest biological, linguistic and cultural relatives of the Eskimo, and we suspect that these two people diverged from a single ancestral population at some time in the past. For convenience, we might call this hypothetical ancestral population "Eskaleut," implying that they were ancestral to both Eskimos and Aleuts. Perhaps the people who lived at Anangula between 8500 and 7000 years ago *were* Eskaleuts.

If we believe that Eskaleuts lived on the Aleutian Islands 8500 years ago, then it is possible that ancestral Eskimos derived from this population and developed their own distinctive language and culture after moving into a neighbouring area.

Scheme I

About 10 000 Years Ago

Original migration of ancestral Eskaleut people from Asia, across the shrinking land bridge.

A. Some of these people moved along the Pacific coast and adapted to maritime conditions. Their remains are found at Anangula by 7500 years ago.

B. Related groups moved across the interior and adapted to tundra hunting and living conditions. Their remains are found in the interior of Alaska by 10 000 years ago.

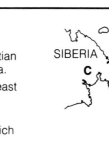

5000-3000 Years Ago

A. The Pacific coast people had developed into ancestral Aleuts on the Aleutian Islands. Aleuts or related people also lived along the south coast of Alaska.

B. The interior people developed the Arctic Small Tool tradition and spread east from Alaska to occupy arctic Canada and Greenland. These people were ancestral Eskimos.

C. Siberia was occupied by Neolithic people, the descendants of groups which had stayed in Asia when their relatives crossed to Alaska. There was little contact across Bering Strait.

3000-1000 Years Ago

A. Aleuts still occupied the Aleutian Islands, but the related populations of South Alaska had disappeared or had been submerged by Eskimo immigration.

B. Alaskan Eskimos developed maritime hunting techniques and spread to Siberia (by 2000 years ago), and to South Alaska, Canada and Greenland (by 1000 years ago). Previous occupants of these areas were displaced or submerged by the Eskimo immigrants.

C. Siberia was occupied by the descendants of Neolithic people, remote relatives of the Eskimos.

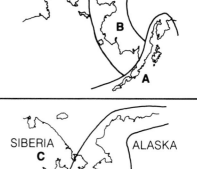

Diagram 2. Four Alternative Schemes of Eskimo Prehistory

Scheme II

About 10 000 Years Ago

A. Original migration of ancestral Aleuts and perhaps other related populations from Asia, across the shrinking land bridge.

B. Ancestral Eskimos remained in Asia after their relatives had crossed to Alaska, and developed a Siberian Neolithic culture.

5000-3000 Years Ago

A. The descendants of the people who crossed to Alaska about 10 000 years ago continued to live along the south coast, where they were ancestral to the Aleuts. The remainder of Alaska was inhabited by Indians.

B. Ancestral Eskimos with an Arctic Small Tool tradition culture, based on the Siberian Neolithic culture, crossed Bering Strait and spread east to occupy arctic Canada and Greenland.

C. Siberia continued to be occupied by related Neolithic populations.

3000-1000 Years Ago

A. Aleuts still occupied the Aleutian Islands, but the related populations of South Alaska had disappeared or had been submerged by Eskimo immigration.

B. Alaskan Eskimos developed maritime hunting techniques and spread to Siberia (by 2000 years ago), and to South Alaska, Canada and Greenland (by 1000 years ago). Previous occupants of these areas were displaced or submerged by the Eskimo immigrants.

C. Siberia was occupied by the descendants of Neolithic people, remote relatives of the Eskimos.

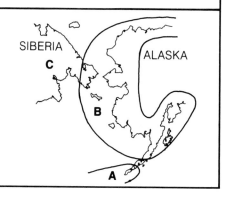

Scheme III

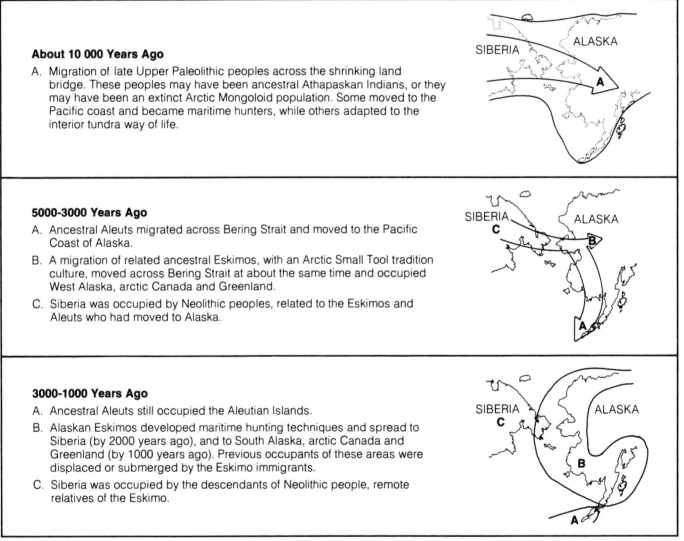

About 10 000 Years Ago

A. Migration of late Upper Paleolithic peoples across the shrinking land bridge. These peoples may have been ancestral Athapaskan Indians, or they may have been an extinct Arctic Mongoloid population. Some moved to the Pacific coast and became maritime hunters, while others adapted to the interior tundra way of life.

5000-3000 Years Ago

A. Ancestral Aleuts migrated across Bering Strait and moved to the Pacific Coast of Alaska.

B. A migration of related ancestral Eskimos, with an Arctic Small Tool tradition culture, moved across Bering Strait at about the same time and occupied West Alaska, arctic Canada and Greenland.

C. Siberia was occupied by Neolithic peoples, related to the Eskimos and Aleuts who had moved to Alaska.

3000-1000 Years Ago

A. Ancestral Aleuts still occupied the Aleutian Islands.

B. Alaskan Eskimos developed maritime hunting techniques and spread to Siberia (by 2000 years ago), and to South Alaska, arctic Canada and Greenland (by 1000 years ago). Previous occupants of these areas were displaced or submerged by the Eskimo immigrants.

C. Siberia was occupied by the descendants of Neolithic people, remote relatives of the Eskimo.

Four Alternative Schemes of Eskimo Prehistory (continued)

Scheme IV

About 10 000 Years Ago

A. Original migration of ancestral Eskaleut people from Asia. These people moved along the Pacific coast and adapted to maritime conditions.

B. A separate migration across the interior brought people who adapted to tundra hunting and living conditions. These people may have been Indians or Arctic Mongoloids.

5000-3000 Years Ago

A. The Pacific coast peoples in the Aleutians area had developed into ancestral Aleuts.

B. The related peoples who had settled the south coast of Alaska had developed into ancestral Eskimos.

C. Siberian Neolithic peoples, probably Arctic Mongoloids who spoke languages related to Eskaleut or Chukotan, crossed Bering Strait and brought with them an Arctic Small Tool tradition culture. These people spread east to occupy arctic Canada and Greenland.

3000-1000 Years Ago

A. Ancestral Aleuts still occupied the Aleutian Islands.

B. Ancestral Eskimos, with maritime hunting techniques developed along the Pacific coast, adapted these techniques to frozen seas and moved northward, displacing or submerging the ASTt occupants of Alaska. By 2000 years ago, they had reached Siberia, and by 1000 years ago, they had moved east to arctic Canada and Greenland.

C. Siberia was occupied by the descendants of Neolithic people, remote relatives of the Eskimos.

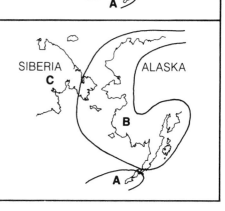

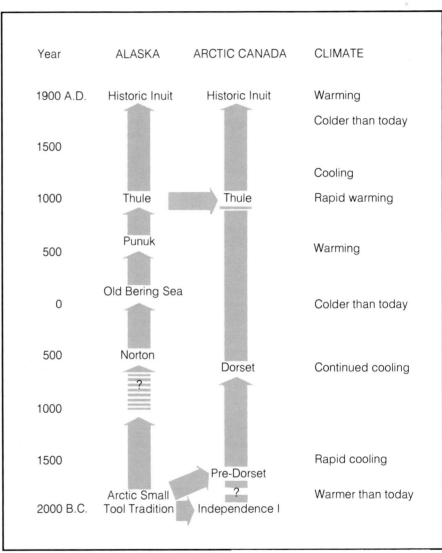

Diagram 3. Summary of Canadian Eskimo Prehistory

The Pacific coast of Alaska is geographically close to the Aleutians, quite similar in environment, and in the historic period was the home of the most densely concentrated Eskimo populations. Perhaps it is here, in the relatively warm and animal-rich environment of South Alaska, that we should search for the development of the Eskimos from an ancestral Eskaleut population and way of life.

Archaeological work on the Alaska Peninsula and on Kodiak Island shows that the southern coast of Alaska was occupied as early as 6000 years ago, by people whose technology somewhat resembled that found at the contemporaneous Anangula Village site. From that time to the present, there are traces of continuous occupation of South Alaska and enough similarity in the archaeological cultures to suggest that the area was occupied continuously by the ancestors of the local South Alaskan Eskimos.

We run into problems, however, when we try to trace the relationships between these early South Alaskan cultures and those in the rest of arctic North America. The first people to occupy the tundras and seasonally frozen coasts of West Alaska, North Alaska, Arctic Canada and Greenland left archaeological remains that are completely different from those of early Aleutian and South Alaskan cultures. These remains are known to archaeologists as the Arctic Small Tool tradition (ASTt), named for the remarkably small size of their chipped-stone tools and weapons. The ASTt people are considered by most archaeologists to have been "the first Eskimos." They were certainly the first people to develop a way of life adapted to those arctic regions inhabited by Eskimos during the historic period. The few known skeletons of ASTt people indicate that they were Arctic Mongoloids, as are the Eskimos and Aleuts and the peoples of northeastern Siberia. There is no way of knowing whether or not they spoke an Eskimo language.

The remains of ASTt camps appear suddenly about 4000 years ago in western and northern Alaska and across arctic Canada to Greenland. The similarity of initial dates across this vast area suggests a population expansion or a migration that occurred rapidly across arctic North America but whose origin is unknown. Some archaeologists suggest that the ASTt developed from the culture of ancient microblade-using peoples who lived in interior Alaska some 10 000 years ago, but this area seems to have been occupied by Indians between about 8000 and 4000 years ago. It is more likely that the ASTt people migrated across Bering Strait from Siberia between 5000 and 4000 years ago. The Neolithic peoples of Siberia had a somewhat similar technology at that time, and it is tempting to see the ASTt people as a Siberian Neolithic population that moved to Alaska and rapidly developed an adaptation to arctic North America. If we assume that the ASTt people were Eskimos, there are two major problems with this theory. Firstly, it is difficult to explain the close similarity of Eskimos, whose ancestors lived in Siberia until 5000 years ago, to Aleuts, who appear to have been in Alaska for the past 8500 years. Secondly, the archaeological continuity between ASTt and more recent Eskimo cultures is not very clear or convincing.

As an alternative to this scheme, we might suggest that the ASTt people were not ancestral Eskimos but Siberian people who may have spoken a language related to the Eskaleut or Chukotan languages. The Eskimos would then trace their ancestry to South Alaska, as suggested earlier. At some time after 3000 years ago some of these South Alaskans may have moved northwards to the Bering Sea and begun to adapt their maritime way of life to this area of seasonally frozen coasts. This development may have prepared the way for the major expansion of maritime-oriented Eskimo cultures that took place in the past 1000 years.

From what we know at present, any of the four theories of early Eskimo prehistory summarized in Diagram 2 may be correct. The Eskimos may have developed from a population that moved across the Bering land bridge at the close of the last Ice Age, or they may have migrated across Bering Strait as recently as 4000 years ago. For the prehistory of arctic Canada, it makes little difference which theory eventually proves to be correct. The immediate ancestors of the Canadian Inuit are known to have spread eastwards from Alaska within the past 1000 years. Before this movement, arctic Canada was occupied by ASTt people who expanded from Alaska about 4000 years ago. Most archaeologists think that the migrants of this first wave were also Eskimos, but it is equally possible that they were Arctic Mongoloids from Siberia who spoke a language that is now extinct. We do not know if any of these people were alive when the ancestors of the Inuit reached arctic Canada or, if so, whether they contributed anything to the Inuit way of life.

CHAPTER 3

The First Wave

The Arctic Small Tool Tradition (2000–800 B.C.)

Both east and west in the country they found the habitations of men, fragments of boats, and stone artifacts, from which it may be seen that the same kind of people had passed this way as those that inhabited Vinland, whom the Greenlanders call Scraelings.
Islendigabok, twelfth century

The above account is a record of the first archaeological finds made by Europeans in the North American Arctic. When Eric the Red explored Greenland in A.D. 982, he met no living people, but did discover the traces of an earlier occupation. These remains must have been those of people of the Dorset culture, a late phase of the Arctic Small Tool tradition. The ASTt people were the first to occupy the northern tundras and frozen coasts of North America. In arctic Canada the ASTt people are often called Palaeo-Eskimos, although it is not known whether they were Eskimos at all.

The ancestors of these people were probably hunters of the northern forest who, at some time between 3000 and 2000 B.C., developed a way of life that allowed them to become independent of the forest zone. They may have been initially attracted to the area north of the tree line by herds of caribou migrating north each summer. Large numbers of caribou could easily be killed at certain places in the tundra where the migratory herds crowded together in mountain passes or in the fords and narrows of lake systems. Once on the tundra the hunters must have discovered other resources: herds of musk-oxen grazing among the flowers of tundra pastures and seals basking on the sea ice. Musk-oxen and seals remained in the Arctic throughout the winter. If these men could learn to hunt them and to use their skins and fat as protection against the cold, it would not be necessary to retreat to the forest in winter.

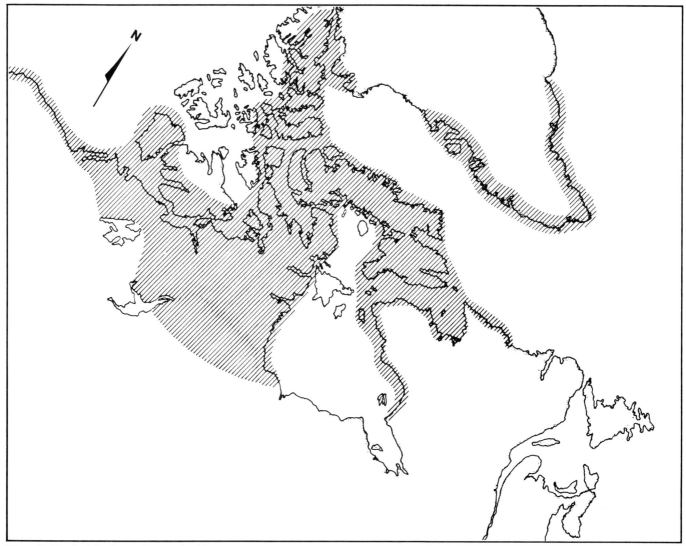

Map 4. Probable Area Occupied by the Arctic Small Tool Tradition

For thousands of years these early hunters must have lived in a northern environment, where they developed a basic technology that could easily be adapted to arctic conditions. They must have had excellent winter clothing, probably made of caribou skins, and tents of the same material. The bow, the spear, and the caribou-hunting skills gained in the northern forest could be effectively used against tundra caribou and musk-oxen. Harpoons of the basic type used at the time by North Pacific sea-mammal hunters or Siberian lake fishermen could have been adapted to the hunting of arctic seals and other sea mammals. The nesting and spawning grounds of many northern species of birds and fish overlap the forest and tundra zones, providing other familiar food sources to people moving north of the tree line. The tree line itself was farther north than at present, and the arctic climate a few degrees warmer than it is today.

This scheme of early ASTt adaptation to arctic conditions is based almost entirely on conjecture, as no archaeological evidence exists. As was mentioned in the last chapter, it is not known whether this initial arctic adaptation was made by Siberian Neolithic peoples of the Chukchi Peninsula, or by Alaskan descendants of the microblade-using peoples who crossed the Bering land bridge about 8000 B.C. ASTt artifacts resemble those of the Siberian Neolithic traditions, but a real ASTt site has yet to be found in Siberia. On the other hand, most of Alaska north of the Pacific coast seems to have been occupied by Indians prior to 2000 B.C., when the first ASTt occupation appeared. The ASTt occupation appeared suddenly, with a technology bearing no relationship to that of the earlier Indian peoples. Relatively little archaeological work has been done in the interior regions of northeastern Siberia, but future work may well show that the transition from a forest Neolithic culture to the tundra-adapted ASTt occurred there.

The earliest-known ASTt sites in Alaska date to about 2000 B.C., and ASTt sites of the same age are known from arctic Canada and Greenland. Since the ancestors of the people of the eastern Arctic must have moved eastwards from Alaska at an earlier time, we may look on them as the true pioneers of arctic life. These were hunters who not only left the shelter of the Siberian or Alaskan forests, but continued to move northwards and eastwards into the coldest, darkest and most barren regions ever inhabited by man.

Two major variants of the early ASTt are found in arctic Canada: the Independence I culture of the High Arctic, and the Pre-Dorset culture of the Low Arctic islands and mainland area. It has been suggested that these cultures represented two groups of people moving eastwards from Alaska at the same time, one heading north toward Greenland and the other east toward Hudson Bay. Although this may be the case, at present it seems more likely that these variants represent two streams of people moving eastwards at different times, or the earlier and later phases of a single stream that lasted for several centuries. The earliest immigrants will be considered here to be those who brought the Independence I culture, and the later group to be those of the Pre-Dorset culture.

Independence I: 2000–1700 B.C.

Between the great ice cap and the northern coast of Greenland lies the region known as Pearyland, a polar desert of gravel and rock intersected by fiords that remain frozen for most or all of the year. Summers are cold and bright, winters extremely cold and dark for several months. Here, along the coasts of Independence Fiord, Eigil Knuth, of the 1948 Danish Pearyland Expedition, discovered the remains of people who had once occupied this most northerly land on earth. The remains were extremely sparse, consisting of tiny stone tools and bone needle fragments scattered in the gravel around the traces of hearths or small tent camps. Most of the sites were located on ancient beaches, which in this area are raised by postglacial uplift to form a series of parallel gravel ridges rising like steps from the present coast. The inhabitants of these sites usually camped on the first beach above the coast of that time, as they probably travelled or hunted on the sea ice. The altitude to which the remains have been raised above the present sea level thus gives us some indication of their age. The hearths and camps with the small stone tools were the highest sites found in the area, and therefore probably the oldest. Some of the hearths contained fragments of charcoal, the remains of fires of local dwarf willow twigs, which have been radiocarbon-dated to about 2000 to 1700 B.C.

Knuth named these traces of the earliest occupation after Independence Fiord, along whose coasts many of the sites were found. Independence I camps are scattered across northern Greenland, and on Ellesmere, Devon and Cornwallis islands in the Canadian High Arctic. Archaeological collections from ASTt sites on Baffin Island and in Labrador contain some stone tools resembling those used by the Independence I people, but the distinctive hearths and camps of the Independence I culture have not been recognized in these Low Arctic regions. This may be because of the difficulty archaeologists have in locating small camps in areas where much of the ground is covered with tundra vegetation.

The remains of an Independence I camp are meagre, usually consisting of a small box-shaped hearth made from slabs of stone set upright in the gravel of an ancient beach. Sometimes the hearth is flanked by two parallel lines of stone slabs, with the gravel on either side smoothed over to make sleeping areas. A narrow rim of gravel or a few small rocks are sometimes found around the periphery of the structure, where they held down the edges of a tent. Such a camp appears to have been used by a single family or, at most, by two small families. The small number of bones and artifacts scattered about most camps suggests that they were usually occupied for only a few days or weeks. Many of the isolated hearths may represent only an overnight stay.

A distinctive feature of Independence I sites is that individual camps are not clustered together, whereas the remains of most camps of arctic hunters are found in compact groups, either around a source of fresh water or in a flat and protected area with access to good hunting or fishing. Such areas appear to have become traditional campsites, used year after year and in some cases over several generations. Old houses were often reoccupied or their stones robbed to build new houses or to hold down the edges of tents. The remains of Independence I camps, however, are found in diffuse strings stretching along a single gravel beach. In the Port Refuge area of Devon Island, over 100 camps were found along 20 kilometres of the ancient beach, some 20 to 22 metres above present sea level. None of these camps appear to have been occupied for more than a few days or weeks, and it seems likely that only one, or at most a few, were occupied at the same time. We can probably conclude that the Independence I people not only preferred to camp at some distance from their neighbours, but also were reluctant to live close to the remains of a camp that had been occupied at an earlier time. Rather than use an old camp, or even rob it of its building materials, they went to considerable trouble to find new stones to build their hearths. We do not know why the Independence I people did this; perhaps they were nervous of old camps or of the ghosts that may have lingered in the vicinity.

Whatever the reason, the resulting dispersed settlement pattern probably explains why Independence I sites have not been recognized in the Canadian Low Arctic or in Alaska. The vegetation that covers most of the land in these areas would easily hide the existence of an Independence I camp, and even if one were discovered accidentally, it probably would not yield enough artifacts to provide definite identification. Independence I camps probably do exist in the Low Arctic and in Alaska, since the chipped-stone artifacts of the culture indicate that it belongs to the ASTt, which likely originated in either Alaska or Siberia.

A prominent feature of the AST tradition, and of Independence I collections, is the use of microblades—the small parallel-sided slivers of flint that were probably used for carving wood and for cutting meat and skins. Another typical artifact is the burin, a distinctive tool made by striking tiny spalls from the edge of a flake and used for cutting bone and other hard materials. The stone tool collections also include several types of points for spears, harpoons and arrows, sideblades that were inserted in the edges of weapons, scrapers used for preparing skins for clothing, and a variety of unidentified artifacts. Although the general forms of these tools indicate an Alaskan ASTt or Siberian Neolithic ancestry, the specific styles of Independence I artifacts are unique.

The ancestors of the Independence I people of the High Arctic must have begun to move eastwards from Alaska at some time between 3000 and 2000 B.C. The movement cannot be seen as a single large migration but, more likely, as a series of small events in which a group of two or three families travelled a few days' distance. The cumulative effect of hundreds of such movements over a period of a few centuries must have resulted in the spread of a scattered population throughout arctic Canada, as far north as Pearyland. The reasons for leaving home probably varied. Some groups or individuals may have moved to areas where previous hunting trips had shown the presence of attractive food resources. Others may have fled the consequences of murders or feuds within the home group. The distinctive dispersed settlement pattern suggests that some people may have moved to a new island because the old one was becoming too heavily populated with the ghosts of dead ancestors.

Palaeoenvironmental studies indicate that in the period before 1500 B.C. arctic Canada was slightly warmer than it is today, and most animal species probably existed in greater numbers than at present. Animals may also have been more easily hunted since they had no previous experience of man. Little is known about the hunting technology of the Independence I people, but what is known suggests that they had weapons capable of taking most arctic animals. The tiny well-made projectile points of chipped flint, with serrated cutting-edges and a basal tang, must have been used as tips for arrows. The remains of bows have not been found, however, and we do not know how powerful and effective the Independence I bow may have been. Larger chipped-stone points appear to have been used to tip spears or lances. Very few harpoon heads have been found, but these appear to be efficient weapons for capturing seals, or even walrus. The forms of the small ivory harpoon heads, with lateral barbs to hold the animal and with a basal tang for mounting the head in the harpoon shaft, recall the harpoons used by North Pacific and Siberian hunters of the time. There is no indication that the Independence I people used boats; their sea hunting may have been done entirely at breathing holes or from the edge of the sea ice. Similarly, no fishing equipment has been preserved, although the fish bones found at several sites show that char and trout were caught by some means.

The remains of other bones found scattered around the camps indicate that a variety of animals were hunted. In northern Greenland and on Ellesmere Island, the Independence I people seem to have been musk-ox hunters. In the Port Refuge area of Devon Island, located close to an area of sea that is ice-free most of the year, a few bones of seal, walrus and polar bear are indications of sea-hunting activities. In comparison with later arctic hunters, however, the Independence I people seem to have depended heavily on small game, such as fox, hare, duck and other waterfowl. Surprisingly, no site has produced much caribou bone, probably indicating that the Independence I people, like the nineteenth-century Polar Eskimos, rarely hunted caribou. Most northern peoples have used caribou skins for winter clothing and tent coverings, as the lightness and warmth of caribou skin make it the most efficient material by far for arctic clothing. We must imagine that the clothing that the Independence I people sewed with their tiny bone needles was made from musk-ox or bear hides, or from the skins of fox, hare and birds.

Tents were perhaps covered with the heavy skin of the musk-ox, supported by poles of driftwood. Their shape is suggested by their outline on the ground, which was rectangular to oval and large enough to house one or two small families. These tents seem to have been used in winter as well as summer; however, the walls of the winter tents may have been insulated with snow blocks. There is no indication that the Independence I people knew how to build the domed snowhouses used by later arctic peoples. In the centre of the tent was an open hearth built of stone slabs, in which were burnt fragments of driftwood scavenged from the beaches, twigs of dwarf willow laboriously gathered from the tundra, and the bones of animals that had been used as food. The small amount of charcoal and burnt bone found around most hearths suggests that fires were small and were used intermittently, perhaps only for cooking. Food may have been roasted, or boiled in containers of wood or skin into which hot stones were dropped. No such containers have been preserved, but stones that seem to have been used for this purpose are found in some hearths. No remains of blubber lamps, stone lamps that burned sea mammal oil, have been found, and the Independence I people probably did not know of this efficient means of heating. A completely closed and insulated dwelling, such as the domed snowhouse, cannot be used with an open fire and is probably a later invention associated with the use of the blubber lamp.

The areas in front of and behind the hearth were often set off from the rest of the dwelling by lines of rock slabs and may have been used for storing food and equipment. On either side of the hearth were sleeping areas, where the gravel had been cleared of its larger stones. The sleeping places were probably covered with skins, and we can assume that the occupants of these unheated tents probably spent a good deal of time keeping warm in bed. During the High Arctic winter, when extreme cold and darkness lasts for several months, the Independence I people may have almost hibernated in their unlit and unheated dwellings.

Little is known of the social life of the Independence I people. The total population was probably very small, and the population density much less than that of later arctic peoples. All of the Independence I camps now known, representing an apparent time span of some three hundred years, could have been left by a single dispersed and mobile band of about a hundred people, although the total population was almost certainly larger than this. The frequency of sites consisting of only one or two tent camps suggests that much of the year was spent wandering about the country in small groups of one or a few families. Larger groups may have gathered occasionally in a good musk-ox hunting or fishing area, but such gatherings were probably of short duration.

The small local groups of Independence I people must have been very vulnerable to starvation when the hunting was poor, or even when one or two hunters were lost through accidents. Extinction of local groups may have occurred frequently, and more-widespread extinctions may have taken place about 1700 B.C., after which time we have little evidence of Independence I occupation in the High Arctic. Perhaps Independence I people continued to live after this time in an archaeologically unknown area. When the Independence II people reoccupied most of the High Arctic after 1000 B.C., they continued to use the old box-hearth, the mid-passage tent, and the dispersed settlement pattern of the Independence I culture. We suspect that somewhere, perhaps in Greenland or on the unexplored islands of Canada's High Arctic, a remnant of the Independence I population continued to live after 1700 B.C. and gave rise to the later Independence II occupation.

Although our archaeological view of Independence I life may be incorrect, the overwhelming picture is one of meagreness—of a people that appear to have accepted a life in which hunger and discomfort were more prevalent than we can imagine from examining the lives of other peoples known through archaeology or ethnology. The lives of later Inuit occupants of the area—people who lived in solid winter houses built of rocks or snow and heated by blubber lamps, and who left deep middens containing the bones of caribou, walrus and whale—appear luxurious by comparison. Yet these first pioneers of the High Arctic, whose lives we would probably consider impossibly meagre and harsh, spent time and energy producing masterpieces in the difficult art of chipping stone tools. The miniature size of their stone artifacts, the use of various brightly coloured flints, and the apparently decorative serration of tool edges suggest that flint chipping was considered an art form and not merely a method of making tools and weapons. This suggests that other aspects of their culture that have not been preserved archaeologically—perhaps their songs or myths or jokes—may also have been important to them and enriched their lives. To the archaeologist who observes the pitifully sparse remains of an Independence I camp, these are happy signs that the people who lived there found their lives enjoyable and worthwhile.

Pre-Dorset: 1700–800 B.C.

Later ASTt occupation of arctic Canada was centred in the region of northern Hudson Bay, Hudson Strait and Foxe Basin. These areas are much richer in game than is the High Arctic, with resources of caribou, fish, birds, resident populations of ringed and bearded seals, migratory harp seals, walrus, and

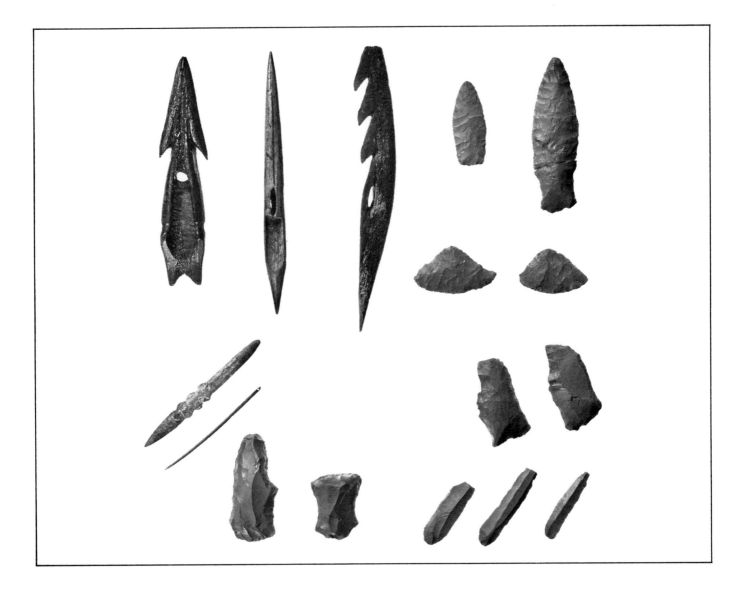

Plate 3. Pre-Dorset Tools and Weapons Pre-Dorset artifacts were made in the same basic tradition as those of the Independence I culture, but there are differences in style as well as some additions to the technology. Clockwise from upper left, these artifacts include: two bone harpoon heads, a barbed bone weapon that may be a fish spear, two flint points for harpoons or spears, two sideblades for mounting in the edges of weapons, two burins for cutting bone, three microblades, two types of flint scraper, a bone needle, and a bone pin of uncertain use.

whales. Little is known of the earliest human occupation of this region, although it was suggested above that Independence I people may have lived there by 2000 B.C.

A large number of early ASTt sites are known from the area, and all have been classified as belonging to the Pre-Dorset culture, ancestral to the later Dorset culture of the eastern Arctic. Pre-Dorset sites have been radiocarbon-dated to as early as 2500 B.C., but the few early dates are suspect. Some were obtained from the charcoal of driftwood, which may have floated for centuries in the arctic ice before being cast up on the beach, and others from burnt seal oil or the bones of sea mammals, which appear to give incorrectly ancient dates. Radiocarbon dates, obtained from the charcoal of local dwarf willows and the bones of land mammals, cluster between roughly 1700 and 800 B.C. and are the dates we shall use arbitrarily to define the Pre-Dorset period.

Although the general forms of early Pre-Dorset artifacts are similar to those of Independence I, there are differences in detail: the microblades are smaller, as are the burins, which are occasionally ground or polished on one surface; the weapon points, sideblades and scrapers are shaped some-what differently; and the technique by which chipped-stone tools were made changes slightly. In all of these characteristics, Pre-Dorset artifacts resemble those known from western Alaska, which date to about 2000 B.C. Small bands of Alaskan ASTt people may have begun to move eastwards at this time, taking with them a more developed technology than that of the earlier Independence I migrants. Spreading to the eastern Arctic within a few centuries, they may have found this area abandoned by its original occupants, or they may have met Independence I people, who then adopted the new technology.

Colour Plate I. An Independence I Camp On the north coast of Devon Island, a box of stone slabs on an empty beach marks the remains of a hearth built about 4000 years ago. An Independence I family may have slept around the hearth, or perhaps just cooked a meal there while travelling.

Whatever the early history of the Pre-Dorset people, they were established over much of the eastern Low Arctic by at least 1700 B.C., and appear to have had a more efficient adaptation and a richer economy than the Independence I people.

The population was also probably larger by this time. Pre-Dorset sites are much more common than Independence I sites, are considerably larger, and have much denser concentrations of bone refuse and discarded artifacts. The remains of individual camps are clustered together in camping areas that appear to have been used seasonally over several generations. Many such areas contain the remains of several dozen structures, and small sites consisting of only one or two camps are rarely found.

The forms of dwellings also appear to have changed at this time. The archaeological remains of Pre-Dorset structures are oval to circular in outline, and are often surrounded by a ring of boulders that held down the edges of a tent. The presence of scattered charcoal and burnt bone indicates that the tents were heated by an interior fire, but we do not find the specialized stone box-hearth and mid-passage of Independence I structures. Small, circular soapstone lamps have been found, which must have been used to burn blubber to provide light and a small amount of heat. The invention of the blubber lamp made possible the use of the domed snowhouse. Circular patches of refuse are found on sites near Igloolik and on Devon Island. These obviously represent remains from the interior of dwellings, but there are no rims of gravel or boulders. These patches may represent the archaeological remains of snowhouses built on the beach, although no specialized snow knives have been found. Snowhouses would have made it possible for people to live on the sea ice during the winter, and this

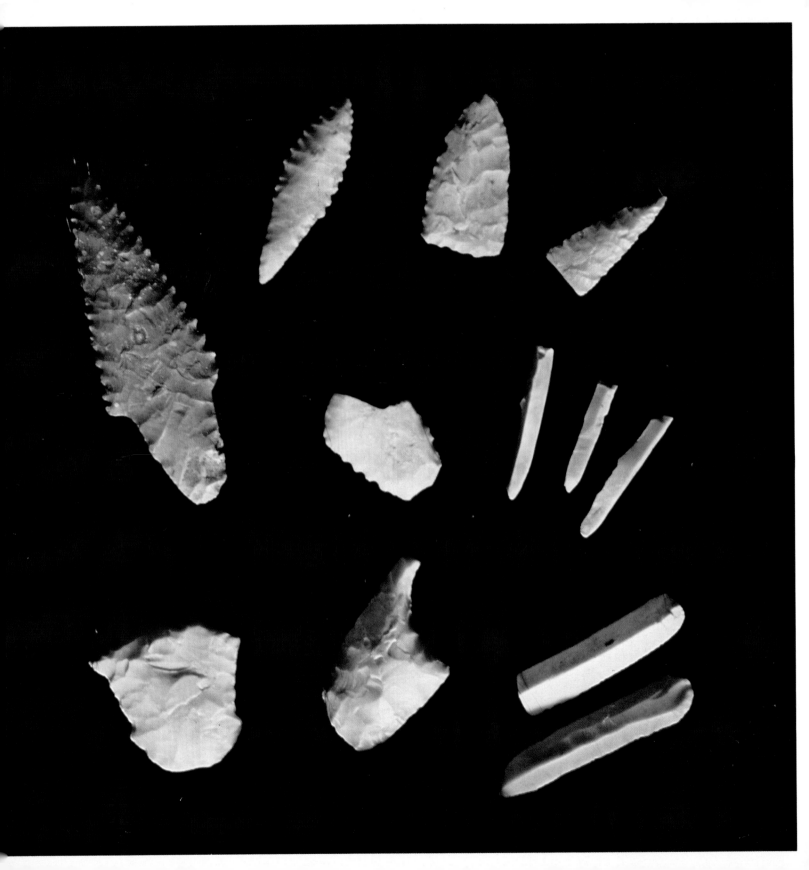

Colour Plate II. The Miniature Tools and Weapons of the Independence I People The earliest occupants of the High Arctic were skilled craftsmen who seem to have delighted in making jewel-like artifacts from brightly coloured flint. The upper row includes four points for spears, arrows or harpoons; in the centre are a miniature burin and three spalls struck from larger burins; in the bottom row are two scrapers used for working hides or for carving, and a pair of microblades that may have been used as small knives. The spear point at upper left is only 5 centimetres long.

would have opened to occupation large areas of the Central Arctic where the ringed seal is the only winter resource.

Other aspects of Pre-Dorset technology show similar progress toward a more efficient adaptation to arctic Canada. Although no parts of boats have been found, the location of sites and the large numbers of sea mammals killed in some areas suggest that boats may have been used, perhaps skin-covered boats of the kayak type. The bones of large dogs have been found at a few sites, but not the specialized sled equipment of later periods; the dogs may have been used for hunting and perhaps for packing. The bow fragments found indicate that a bow strengthened by a cable of braided sinew was used, perhaps of about the same efficiency as that used by later Inuit hunters. Lances, with heads of bone, insets for flint points and oval, flint sideblades, could also be used for hunting most large mammals. Barbed antler prongs appear to have belonged to fish spears or bird spears. Pre-Dorset sites are often found at the same fishing and caribou-hunting localities used by later peoples. It seems likely that fish weirs and caribou drive-fences found in these locations were first built by the Pre-Dorset people.

Harpoon equipment also appears to have changed at that time. The earliest-known Pre-Dorset harpoon heads have basal sockets for inserting a foreshaft. These "female" harpoon heads were made on a completely different principle than the "male" harpoon heads of the Independence I culture, which had a basal tang for mounting into a cup-shaped socket on the harpoon shaft. The Pre-Dorset socketed harpoons are of the toggling type with sharp basal spurs; when driven into a sea mammal, these spurs catch inside the skin and toggle the harpoon head sideways across the wound, providing a more secure grip than can be obtained with barbs.

**Plate 4. The Remains of a
Pre-Dorset House**   A circular
depression in the gravel marks
the site of a tent or perhaps a
snowhouse. The vegetation growing
within the structure is feeding on
nutrients from refuse left on the
house floor over 3500 years ago.

The socketed, toggling harpoon head has usually been considered a distinctive characteristic of Eskimo technology. It is interesting, therefore, to find that it may have been invented elsewhere and introduced to the Arctic during Pre-Dorset times. Recent archaeological finds in southern Labrador have indicated that the Maritime Archaic Indians of the area were using socketed, toggling harpoon heads at least as early as 5000 B.C. Harpoon heads found in the Maritime Archaic cemetery at Port au Choix, Newfoundland, which is dated to about 2000 B.C., are similar to those from early Pre-Dorset sites in the eastern Arctic. At Saglek Bay in northern Labrador, both Maritime Archaic and ASTt occupations are dated to about 2000 B.C., and it is possible that the ASTt people learned of the toggling harpoon head through contact with their Indian neighbours. At the same time, it has been suggested that the ASTt people may have introduced the bow and arrow to the Archaic Indians. Small stone weapon points, which may have been used to tip arrows, begin to appear in Labrador Indian sites of this period, possibly the earliest-known arrow points from American Indian sites. Brief contacts along the northern coast of Labrador may have resulted in the spread of the Indian harpoon head across the Arctic, where it became an essential element of Eskimo technology. Meanwhile, the Siberian-based ASTt bow and arrow spread southwards to become the main weapon of most Indian groups.

The styles of Pre-Dorset harpoon heads changed gradually over time, changes that the archaeologist finds useful in placing sites in temporal sequence. From large sites in the Igloolik area, the correlation of harpoon head styles with radiocarbon dates and with the elevations of beaches on which the specimens were found has allowed the construction of a continuous sequence of style changes from earliest Pre-Dorset times to

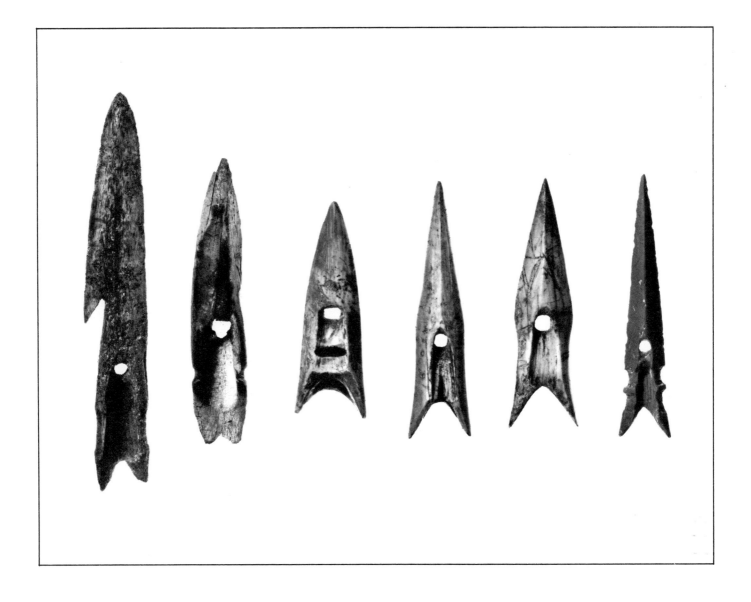

Plate 5. Style Changes in Pre-Dorset and Dorset Harpoon Heads Harpoons were the most important weapons of most early hunters in arctic Canada. Just as we change the styles of our automobiles from year to year, they changed the styles of their harpoon heads from generation to generation. Archaeologists can trace these style changes through time and use them to give a rough date to associated artifacts. The harpoon heads shown here are from various periods, ranging from about 1700 B.C. on the left to about A.D. 1000 on the right.

the latest Dorset sites of A.D. 800. The harpoon was probably the most important weapon in the arsenal of most Pre-Dorset hunters. It could have been used to kill ringed seals at their breathing holes and to harpoon swimming seals, walrus, and occasionally small whales, such as the beluga and narwhal. Bone refuse found at various sites indicates that seal and walrus were the most important animals hunted in the Pre-Dorset core area of northern Hudson Bay, Hudson Strait and Foxe Basin. Although caribou, fish and birds were also taken, it was probably the sea-mammal resources that allowed continuous occupation of the area throughout the Pre-Dorset and subsequent Dorset periods.

We can only roughly estimate the size of Pre-Dorset populations in the core area. The total was probably somewhat smaller than that of the historic Inuit of the area, somewhere between 1000 and 3000 persons. Bands of perhaps a hundred may have camped together during certain seasons at traditional fishing spots, caribou crossings, and seal- or walrus-hunting grounds. But during much of the year, these bands probably split into smaller groups and moved about the country to exploit different resources. Although some of the local bands may have occasionally died through accident or starvation, immigration from neighbouring bands was probably sufficient to make up these losses.

Outside the core area the picture is not one of continuous occupation, but of sporadic immigration, occupation and extinction. Most of the movements into peripheral regions probably originated in the core area. For various reasons a local camp group or band may have moved into an unoccupied region and adapted to the specific resources there. These local populations then appear to have expanded, perhaps in some cases to several hundred people, but none seem to have survived for longer than a few centuries. Palaeoenvironmental studies show that the Pre-Dorset period was the closing phase of the postglacial warm period, and that the climate was becoming cooler. The tree line retreated southwards, beyond its present position. The sea ice may have become heavier and longer lasting, and the populations and ranges of many animal species were probably reduced. Occupation of peripheral areas may have been perilous under these deteriorating conditions, as most of the inhabitants depended upon a more limited range of resources than existed in the core area.

In Labrador, occupation seems to have occurred early in the Pre-Dorset sequence. Little is known of this occupation, as few sites and no preserved bone or wood have been found. Sites occur as far south as Nain. The Labrador Pre-Dorsets probably had a mixed economy that combined hunting sea mammals along the coast with autumn hunting of caribou in the interior. The few radiocarbon dates available and the early styles of the artifacts suggest that the occupation may have ended before 1500 B.C.

The High Arctic north of Parry Channel has yielded few Pre-Dorset sites. Definite occupation has been established only for Devon Island, but there are hints that people may have lived as far north as the Thule district of northwestern Greenland. The artifacts from the Cape Sparbo and Port Refuge sites on Devon Island appear to belong to a very early period in the Pre-Dorset stylistic sequence, and sites are found at elevations only slightly lower than those of nearby Independence I sites. At Port Refuge the people seem to have lived by coastal sealing, although caribou and birds were hunted as well. Again, the occupation of the High Arctic may have been brought to an end by the deteriorating environmental conditions that began about 1500 B.C.

On the islands of the Central Arctic we see a different picture. Although early ASTt people must have lived in this region during their slow progress from Alaska to the eastern Arctic, no definite traces have been found. Only at a small site on the Dismal Lakes, northeast of Great Bear Lake, do we find a few artifacts that may relate to the original migration. All other Pre-Dorset sites in the area seem to date to between roughly 1500 and 900 B.C., and represent an adaptation quite different from that of the core area. The known sites in this region were occupied by people who were engaged primarily in hunting land mammals or fishing. At the Umingmak site on northern Banks Island, the bones of hundreds of musk-oxen are scattered over a large area and occur in conjunction with Pre-Dorset artifacts. These bones must represent many kills, probably by a small band of hunters over several generations. At sites near Wellington Bay on the south coast of Victoria Island, caribou were the main quarry. Lines of stone markers, built as drive-fences to funnel migrating caribou toward the hunters, lie along many ridges in the area; some of these may have been built originally by the Pre-Dorsets. At Bloody Falls, 15 kilometres above the mouth of the Coppermine River, a small Pre-Dorset site likely represents the remains of a summer camp occupied by people fishing for char, which collect in large numbers below the falls. All of these sites may have been occupied during the summer and autumn; however, no definite winter occupation sites have been found. Although it may have been possible for the people of Banks Island to hunt musk-oxen throughout the year, the caribou hunters of Victoria Island and the fishermen of Bloody Falls must have spent the winter on the sea ice, perhaps living in snowhouses. This pattern of life was probably not very different from that of the Inuit who occupied the area in historic times.

To the south of this region lie the Barren Grounds, the great tundra triangle between the Central Arctic coast and Hudson Bay. Traditionally the Barren Grounds have been Indian territory, occupied since at least 6000 B.C. by caribou hunters who moved northwards from the tree line each summer. Traces of Indian occupation disappear about 1500 B.C., however, and for the following 700 years the area was occupied by Pre-Dorset caribou hunters. Their artifacts, including small burins, rare microblades, and small triangular arrow points made of chipped and occasionally ground flint, resemble those used by the Pre-Dorset people of the Central Arctic coast. It is possible to imagine caribou hunters of the Coronation Gulf region deciding not to remain on the coast to hunt seals during the winter, but rather to follow the caribou on their southward migration and to spend the winter near or within the northern forest.

Pre-Dorset sites of this kind are found around the Colville lakes, Great Bear and eastern Great Slave lakes, and perhaps as far south as Lake Athabaska. To the east they are found along the Coppermine and Thelon rivers and along the rivers of northern Manitoba draining to Hudson Bay. Little is known about these interior Pre-Dorset people because only stone tools, charcoal from their hearths and a small quantity of bone have been found preserved on their sites. They may have been the first ASTt people to adapt completely to an interior way of life and to become independent of the sea-mammal hunting to which their ancestors had adapted a millennium earlier. Their appearance in the Barren Grounds and apparently in the forests as far south as northern Saskatchewan and Manitoba may have been partly a result of the same climatic cooling that probably caused the Pre-Dorset people to abandon the High Arctic. About 1500 B.C. there were major forest fires in the Barren Grounds, and the tree line retreated southwards, never regaining its previous position. It has been suggested that a cooling climate may have killed much of the northern forest close to the tree line, making it susceptible to extensive forest fires. Whatever the cause, such an event must have disrupted caribou migrations and, consequently, the lives of Indian hunters. This may in turn have opened the way for the Pre-Dorset occupation of the Barren Grounds. The occupation was only temporary, however, as no interior Pre-Dorset sites have been dated later than 800 B.C. By this time, Indians appear to have established themselves once more in the Barren Grounds, as far north as Bloody Falls on the Coppermine River.

The Pre-Dorset people of the Barren Grounds probably became extinct because their major resource, the caribou, proved too undependable in the long run. Arctic hunters who specialize in the pursuit of a single species have a precarious existence, at the mercy of uncontrollable factors such as sudden climatic changes and forest fires. If, for example, the caribou do not arrive in the expected area at the expected time, or the fish do not return to a particular river, or the sea freezes a few weeks later than the time when people expect to begin their winter sealing, a band may die of starvation. If these unexpected events occur often enough, the population of an entire region may become extinct. In this way the Pre-Dorset hunters of the Barren Grounds, together with their relatives in the High Arctic several centuries earlier, may have disappeared. Only in the species-rich core area of Foxe Basin, Hudson Strait and northern Hudson Bay do we find Pre-Dorset people surviving after 800 B.C. Here, new technological elements were combined to form the Dorset culture. Its alien character has intrigued archaeologists for decades.

CHAPTER 4

Tunit

The Dorset Culture (800 B.C.–A.D. 1000)

The Tunit were a strong people, and yet they were driven from their villages by others who were more numerous, by many people of great ancestors; but so greatly did they love their country that when they were leaving Uglit there was a man who, out of desperate love for his village, harpooned the rocks with his harpoon and made the stones fly about like bits of ice.
Ivaluardjuk, Igloolik area, 1922

According to legend, the Tunit were a large and gentle race, great hunters of seals, whom the ancestors of the Inuit encountered on moving into the Canadian Arctic. After living together peacefully for some time, the two peoples quarrelled, and the Tunit were driven away. Inuit mythology tells of many strange races, human and subhuman, that inhabited the arctic world. The stories about the Tunit stand out, however, because the race is described in detail and specific localities are known as places where the Tunit lived. It seems probable that these stories relate to an actual ancient race that occupied arctic Canada when the first Inuit arrived.

Archaeological evidence for the existence of such a race was first recognized in 1925, when Diamond Jenness, of the National Museum of Canada, received a collection of artifacts from Cape Dorset in southern Baffin Island. Realizing that these artifacts were unlike any known from the recent history of the Inuit, Jenness suggested that they represented a more ancient way of life, which he named the Dorset culture. More recent work has shown that the Dorset culture was a widespread phenomenon, at one time occupying most of arctic Canada east of Dolphin and Union Strait, north to Greenland, and south to Newfoundland. Dorset remains are found throughout this

Plate 6. Independence II Tools and Weapons   Independence II artifacts do not resemble those of the earlier Independence I and Pre-Dorset cultures but are related to those of the more recent Dorset culture. Some Dorset artifacts may have derived their styles from Independence II prototypes. Clockwise from upper left, these include: a bone harpoon head, two chipped-stone knives or points for spears, a sideblade for a weapon, a skin-scraper, a ground-flint burin-like tool, a ground-stone adze blade, two microblades, and a microblade core.

Plate 7. An Independence II Tent Foundation   Built of small stone slabs, this Devon Island ruin shows the characteristic form of Independence structures: the central passage with box-shaped hearth and the two sleeping areas, the whole surrounded by the stones that held down the edges of the tent. The structure has not been excavated. It is in the same condition it was left in by its builders 2500 to 3000 years ago.

area, often well preserved in the permafrost of deep middens, but they are tantalizingly inadequate for reconstructing the way of life of the Dorset people.

Some have speculated that the Dorset people were Indians who migrated northwards to the eastern Arctic, or at least were heavily influenced by Archaic Indian cultures of northeastern North America. Further work has shown this to be incorrect, and we can now trace the main lines of Dorset development from the Pre-Dorset culture of the core area of northern Hudson Bay, Hudson Strait and Foxe Basin. This development seems to have occurred between 1000 and 500 B.C. Before we trace its history, we shall look briefly at a Dorset-like culture that seems to have existed in the High Arctic during the earliest stages of Dorset development in the core area.

Independence II: 1000–500 B.C.

The rock and gravel barrens of northern Greenland and the Canadian High Arctic appear to have been abandoned by the Independence I people about 1700 B.C. Aside from two Pre-Dorset sites, there are few traces of habitation in the region for several centuries until perhaps 1000 B.C., when another major but poorly dated occupation occurred. The remains of this culture were discovered by Eigil Knuth on beaches at lower elevations than the earliest Independence I sites, and he named the culture Independence II.

The area of known Independence II occupation—Cornwallis, Bathurst, Devon and Ellesmere islands and the Peary-land region of northern Greenland—is approximately the same as that of Independence I, and some characteristics suggest a close link between the two cultures. This link is visible in the settlement pattern: Independence II camps are found in the long, dispersed strings that are characteristic of Independence I settlement. The form of dwelling is also similar: rectangular to oval in outline, with a central box-hearth flanked by two lines of vertical slabs that form a mid-passage with gravel sleeping areas on either side. Somewhere in Greenland or in the High Arctic, people must have continued to build this style of dwelling since Independence I times.

The artifacts found in Independence II sites, however, are distinctly different in style from those of the earlier period. The few harpoon heads found are identical to late Pre-Dorset forms from the Igloolik sites, which date to about 1000 B.C. Similarly, the bone lance heads with flint sideblades resemble late Pre-Dorset lances from the core area. Flint weapon points and knives have wide side-notches for hafting, a trait that is not known in either Independence I or Pre-Dorset cultures. Microblades continue to be used, but burins have been replaced by "burin-like tools" made by grinding the flint after chipping it. The small, cylindrical bone needles with round eyes used by earlier ASTt people have now been replaced by larger, flat needles with elongated, gouged eyes. Fragments of oval and rectangular soapstone bowls or lamps have been found at one site.

Most of these traits are characteristic of core area Dorset culture in the period after 800 B.C. Because of this, Independence II has been generally considered to be merely a northern variant of Dorset culture. Two features of Independence II culture hint, however, at a somewhat different interpretation. The first is that the styles of Independence II harpoon heads, the most sensitive indicators of ASTt cultural development, are the same as those of the core area Pre-Dorset culture, which

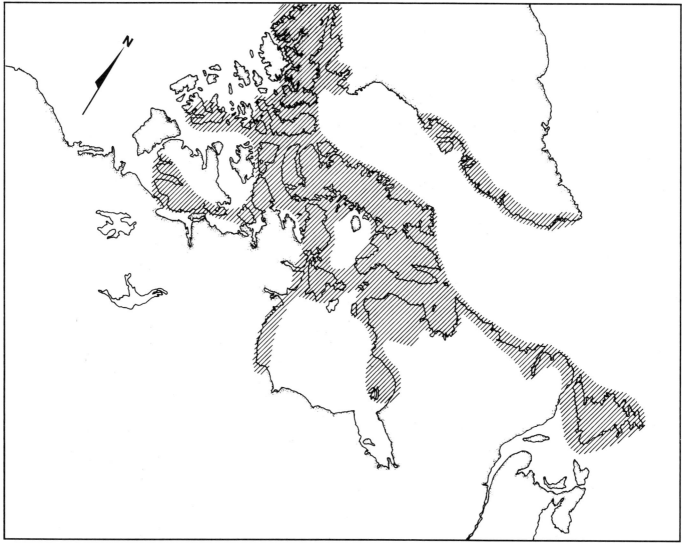

Map 5. Probable Area Occupied by the Dorset Culture

Colour Plate III. The Equipment of a Dorset Shaman? These objects were recovered from a small Dorset village on Dundas Island in the High Arctic. They include: a small wooden figure of a human, the hole in the chest containing a sliver of wood; an ivory carving of a bird, probably a ptarmigan; a miniature harpoon head; a spectacle-shaped ivory carving; two bear-headed spatulas; a small wooden carving of a bear, which was found in a crack in bedrock behind the village; and a double-pointed wooden object. The use of these objects is not known, but many are of standard types and may have been used by magicians.

are several centuries older than the styles associated with early Dorset culture. The second is the inference that the characteristic Dorset house, rectangular in outline, with central hearth and mid-passage flanked by two sleeping areas, is derived from the old Independence I type of dwelling. It seems possible that other elements of Dorset culture—such as the side-notched flint points, the rectangular and oval soapstone bowls or lamps, the ground-flint burin-like tools, and the flat needles with elongated eyes—were developed in the High Arctic during the second millennium B.C. and were later introduced to the people of the core area.

Dorset: 800 B.C.–A.D. 1000

Throughout the Pre-Dorset sequence in the core area, styles of artifacts changed rather slowly. Harpoon heads were gradually modified toward closed-socket forms; flint burins were ground and polished more frequently; flint weapon points changed in form; and ground-slate points appeared occasionally in more recent sites. In the period between 1000 and 500 B.C., these processes of change continued and, according to one interpretation of the rather confused radiocarbon dates from this period, may have accelerated. In the same period, new styles of dwellings began to be built, more microblades were made, flint knives and weapon points were made with side-notches for hafting, oval and rectangular soapstone pots or lamps appeared, and burins were replaced by ground-flint burin-like tools. Snow knives and sled shoes (ivory plates attached to the runners of sleds to protect them on rough ice) appeared, suggesting a new adaptation to winter hunting on the sea ice. At the same time, evidence for bow-hunting decreased. The cumulative effect of these changes produced, by some time

**Colour Plate IV. Ivory Weapons
of the Old Bering Sea Culture**
These ivory artifacts, stained from
lying in the earth for about 2000
years, were made by the first
Eskimos to develop an efficient
maritime adaptation to the Bering Sea
area. All appear to be hunting
weapons, and their extensive
decoration may have been magically
useful in capturing sea mammals.
The butterfly-shaped object may be a
harpoon rest that was once mounted
on the stem of an umiak.

earlier than 500 B.C., the way of life known as the Dorset
culture.

Some of these new technological elements may have been
invented locally, but some may have been introduced from
other areas. It was once thought that the Dorset people learned
to make ground-slate tools, side-notched weapon points, and
soapstone bowls from Archaic Indian cultures of the northern
forests. This now seems unlikely because the specific styles
of Archaic artifacts that resemble those of the Dorset culture
are now known to have occurred at least one thousand years
earlier than the Dorset styles. Nevertheless, Dorset people
lived in Labrador as early as 700 B.C., where they may have
encountered and been influenced by Indian cultures. Contact
with Eskimo cultures in Alaska cannot be ruled out. No Dorset
sites are known west of Dolphin and Union Strait, nor are sites
of the contemporaneous Alaskan Norton culture known east of
the Mackenzie River; therefore, contact between the two
peoples would appear to have been minimal. However, the
distinctive ground-flint burin-like tools appear in both areas at
about the same time, as do the first semisubterranean houses.
As mentioned previously, the Dorset-like Independence II culture of the High Arctic may date earlier than the beginning of
the Dorset period and, consequently, may have been the origin
of some Dorset traits.

Influences may thus have reached late Pre-Dorset and early
Dorset cultures from several directions, but it is likely that most
of the development occurred in the core area itself. Part of this
development may have taken place in response to environmental change, since palaeoenvironmental studies of arctic
Canada indicate that the climate continued to cool throughout
the early Dorset period, reaching a cold peak just before A.D. 0.

Plate 8. A Dorset Village On the shores of Musk-Ox Fiord, Ellesmere Island, the site of a 1500-year-old village is marked by four patches of vegetation growing in rectangular depressions. Tents or snow-walled houses must have stood over these depressions, giving shelter to an autumn or winter camp of Dorset people.

It is impossible to determine what effects such a change would have had on sea ice and on animal populations. The appearance in early Dorset culture of equipment designed for living and hunting on sea ice may be related to the growing importance of sea-mammal hunting on winter ice, which was more extensive and lasted a greater part of the year.

Whatever the environment, the Dorset adaptation appears to have been richer and more successful than that of their Pre-Dorset ancestors. Dorset sites are larger and more numerous in the core area, and have deeper middens of bone refuse. They are concentrated in northern Foxe Basin, in the Pond Inlet region of northern Baffin Island, on both sides of Hudson Strait, and on the islands of northern Hudson Bay. Throughout this area we may imagine a series of Dorset camp groups, varying in size from place to place and from season to season depending on the food resources available. Artifacts and house styles are similar throughout the core area at any one time, and so far it has been impossible to recognize regional subgroups or "tribes." The total population of the core area was probably higher than in Pre-Dorset times, and may be roughly estimated at between 2000 and 5000.

The seasonal round of activities must have varied according to the environment and resources of each local region. The general pattern in the core area was probably not much different from that of later Inuit inhabitants. Dorset people may have spent spring and summer on the coast, hunting walrus as they hauled themselves out of the sea onto the beach, harpooning seals and walrus from the edge of the landfast ice, and perhaps hunting from kayaks in open water. Later in the summer, larger groups may have gathered at fishing spots where char could be speared and at places where caribou could be hunted. The autumn may have been passed in semisubterranean houses on the coast until the winter ice formed. Some groups may have spent the winter in these houses, living on stored food or hunting in nearby areas of open water, but most Dorset people probably passed the winter in snowhouse communities hunting seals at their breathing holes.

Most of this reconstruction of seasonal activities is based on what we know of Dorset hunting technology, their kinds of dwellings, and the animal bones found at sites. Little is known about their weapons for fishing and for hunting land mammals. For example, it is generally held that the Dorset people did not use the bow and arrow, as no artifacts have been identified definitely as such. The artifacts identified as fish spears are small, delicate, barbed objects that do not appear to have been very efficient. Despite this apparent lack of efficient weapons, Dorset sites are found at fishing stations, and in some areas there is evidence that large numbers of caribou were killed; perhaps these were taken with lances or even with harpoons, as many harpoon heads have been found in some caribou-hunting camps.

Dorset harpoons appear to have been capable of killing seals, walrus, and perhaps small whales such as the narwhal and beluga. The remains of larger whales are found at some sites, but these may have been drift carcasses scavenged from the beaches. There is no evidence of the complex float equipment that made later Inuit harpoons so efficient and allowed the capture of much larger animals. The Dorset harpoon line must have been held in the hand, or was perhaps moored to an ice-chisel jammed into the ice, when walrus were hunted at the floe edge. Such an arrangement must have made the hunting of larger sea mammals a dangerous sport, especially

Plate 9. Dorset Tools and Weapons Compared with their ASTt ancestors, the Dorset people had a rather sophisticated technology. The artifacts illustrated here include, clockwise from upper left: two styles of harpoon heads, perhaps used for different types of hunting; a bone lance; a microblade knife in a composite bone-and-wood handle; a ground-flint burin-like tool in a similar handle; two styles of chipped-stone points, and a ground-slate point; an ivory fish spear; a bone needle; and, at lower left, an ivory ice-creeper designed to be tied beneath the foot to prevent slipping on smooth ice.

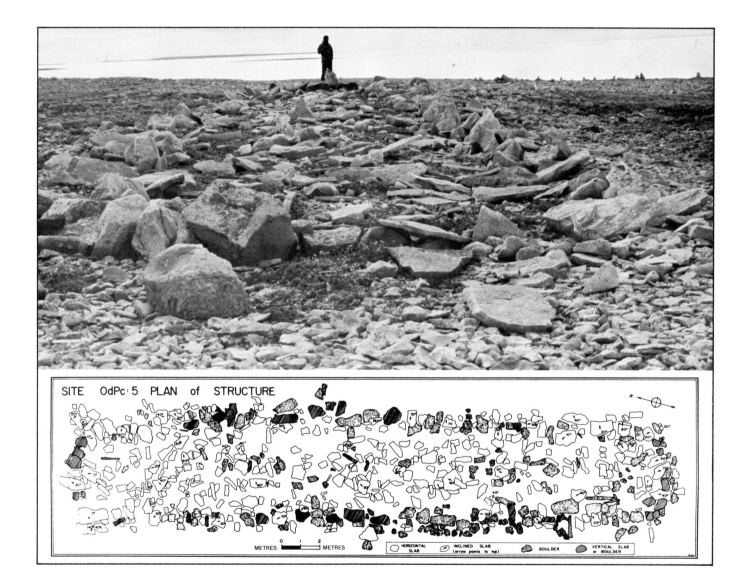

SITE OdPc:5 PLAN of STRUCTURE

METRES 0 1 2 METRES

HORIZONTAL SLAB   INCLINED SLAB (arrow points to top)   BOULDER   VERTICAL SLAB or BOULDER

Plate 10. Photograph and Plan of a Dorset Longhouse This structure, discovered on western Victoria Island in the Central Arctic, is 32 metres long and 7 metres wide, with walls built of large boulders and slabs of stone. The few artifacts found inside suggest that it was built by Dorset people about A.D. 500. There are no indications that it ever had a roof, and it may have been used for some temporary social or ceremonial purpose. Similar structures found in Ungava have been claimed as evidence for a Norse occupation of the area but were probably also built by the Dorset people.

from boats. Our knowledge of Dorset boats is limited to a few carvings that may represent kayaks, and two wooden objects found at Button Point on Bylot Island that appear to be kayak ribs.

Dorset harpoons could also have been used for hunting seals at winter breathing holes, probably an important activity throughout much of the Dorset area. Other adaptations to winter life on the sea ice included sleds, ice-creepers tied under boots to prevent slipping, and perhaps the domed snowhouse. A Dorset toy found on a site near Lake Harbour in southern Baffin Island is a model of a short sled of the komatik type used by the later Inuit. Fragments of ivory sled shoes have also been found. The sleds appear to have been small and were probably pulled by hand, as no artifacts have been identified as dog-sledding equipment. Our only evidence that the Dorset people had dogs consists of a single skull, which may be that of a wolf rather than a dog, found at a Lake Harbour site. Evidence for snowhouses is equally circumstantial and includes blubber lamps and flat bone artifacts suspected of having been used as knives for cutting blocks of snow.

Dorset lamps are much smaller than those used by the recent Inuit and are either oval or rectangular with sloping sides. Some of these objects were cooking pots, but others contain the burnt remains of blubber and must have been used as lamps. Such lamps could have been used to light and heat snowhouses or the more permanent sod-walled winter houses known from several areas. According to Inuit legend, the Tunit placed small lamps under their coats for warmth while waiting for seals at the breathing holes.

Dorset winter houses were semisubterranean (dug several centimetres below ground), generally rectangular in outline, and appear large enough to have housed from two to four small families. The interior arrangements were similar to the Independence II dwellings with a central working or cooking area flanked by two sleeping platforms. Inuit legend claims that the Tunit used sleeping platforms so narrow that they slept with their legs raised against the walls of the house. This story may have arisen from observation of abandoned Dorset dwellings, but it seems more likely that Dorset people slept parallel to the central cooking area rather than at right angles, as is the Inuit practice. The walls of these houses appear to have been built of sod, and perhaps partly of snow blocks. There are usually no traces of wooden or bone roof supports, but the roof must have been covered with skins. Summer tents also appear to have been rectangular, with the same interior arrangement. The remains of tents show a central floor area paved with flagstones and having one or two hearths, which usually contain wood charcoal and burnt blubber. The hearths are flanked by upright stones that probably served to support soapstone cooking pots.

During the first millennium A.D., Dorset people began to build occasional large stone structures, which have been called "longhouses." Perhaps the most famous of these are the three longhouses on Pamiok Island in Ungava Bay, which have been attributed by some to a Greenlandic Norse occupation. The largest of these houses is 25 metres long by 7 metres wide and is surrounded by a wall of slabs and boulders. Dorset artifacts were found within the structures, suggesting that Dorset people either built or occupied them after they were abandoned by the original builders. So far, the only evidence for a possible non-Dorset occupation of Pamiok Island is an iron axe which was found in an Inuit tent ring and which perhaps was excavated from a longhouse by Inuit. Although the evidence from Ungava is not sufficient to confirm that Dorset people built the longhouses, the presence of Dorset remains in the houses is most suggestive. Moreover, similar structures were built by Dorset people near Igloolik and on Victoria and Bathurst islands, areas which the Greenlandic Norse could never have penetrated. The largest known longhouse, found on the north coast of Prince Albert Sound, Victoria Island, is very similar to the Ungava structures, and a Dorset harpoon head was found inside. This structure has heavy stone walls but no remains of a roof. Only a few caribou bones were found in the vicinity, suggesting that the structure was not used as a dwelling.

Outside the Dorset core area, we find the same pattern of sporadic occupation described for the Pre-Dorset period. The northern coast of Labrador may have been an extension of the Dorset core area, as settlement had reached as far south as Nain by 700 B.C. Dorset people may not have penetrated to southern Labrador until a few centuries later, but from there some crossed the Strait of Belle Isle and occupied Newfoundland. For at least a thousand years, between approximately 500 B.C. and A.D. 500., the Dorsets seem to have been the most numerous and perhaps the only occupants of Newfoundland. They developed a distinctive way of life in this, the most southerly area ever occupied by Arctic peoples. Their sites are found around the entire coast of Newfoundland and in the caribou-hunting area of the interior lakes. The largest sites are on the west coast and the Northern Peninsula, where Dorset hunters exploited the herds of harp seals, which give birth to their pups on the spring ice.

The Newfoundland Dorset people had a distinctive burial pattern, placing their dead in small caves or crevices in limestone cliffs. Several skeletons have been found and studied, and these indicate that the Dorset people were Arctic Mongoloid in physical type. This is our only evidence that the Dorset people, as well as their ASTt ancestors, belonged to an Eskimo or Eskimo-like race with Asiatic affinities, rather than to an American Indian race. Dorset burial patterns are almost unknown in arctic regions, where only a few mandibles and longbones have been found in house middens or apparent burial pits.

At some time between A.D. 500 and 1000, the Dorset people ceased to occupy Newfoundland and were replaced by the ancestors of the Beothuk Indians. We do not know whether the Dorsets were killed by the Indians, whether they died out before the Indians arrived, or whether the two groups peacefully shared the island for some time. There may have been contact between the groups, as Beothuk artistic motifs and harpoon head styles show an intriguing resemblance to those of the Dorset culture. We have no evidence that the two groups intermarried; the few known Beothuk skeletons indicate that these people were American Indian in racial type, with no evidence of Arctic Mongoloid ancestry.

In the High Arctic, the only Dorset sites known are those of the later phases, which have been roughly dated to between A.D. 500 and 1000. Earlier remains, which have been identified as Dorset, are known from West Greenland, but these may derive from the local "Sarqaq" ASTt variant or from the Independence II culture of northern Greenland. High Arctic Canada may have been habitable only during the period of warming climate after A.D. 500, and, as in Newfoundland, High Arctic Dorset culture had probably disappeared by A.D. 1000.

On the islands of the Central Arctic there were two waves of Dorset occupation, which apparently originated in migrations from the core area. The first wave, between 500 B.C. and A.D. 100, occupied sites on King William Island near Cambridge Bay, the Ekalluk River in southern Victoria Island, and Prince Albert Sound in western Victoria Island. These sites were occupied by caribou hunters and river fishermen, who must have spent the winters sealing from the ice. Unlike the Pre-Dorset occupation of the Central Arctic, the Dorset people barely penetrated the mainland coast or the Barren Grounds; only one small site has been found on the mainland side of Dolphin and Union Strait. Evidence exists that Indians occupied the Barren Grounds at this time, as far north as Bloody Falls on the Coppermine River, and their presence may have prevented Dorset people from inhabiting the mainland. The Dorset occupation of the Central Arctic seems to have ceased by A.D. 100, and we have only slight evidence of a later reoccupation between A.D. 500 and 1000.

Dorset culture attained its greatest expansion during this late period, when it extended from southeastern Hudson Bay to northwestern Greenland, and as far west as Victoria and Melville islands. It was also during this phase that Dorset art appears to have reached its peak. Small carved objects of wood, bone and ivory are known from Dorset sites of all periods but are most commonly found on sites of this late period. Dorset art has been described as a magical art form, intimately connected with shamanistic activities. The importance of shamanism and witchcraft are suggested by finds of wooden masks, sets of carved animal teeth made to fit into performer's mouths, and drums that may have been used by the shaman. Many carvings of bears and of men have a hole in the chest or throat, often containing a splinter of wood or a patch of red ochre. Carved bone tubes may have been used by the shaman to suck illness from the body, and miniature harpoon heads may have been magic weapons. Small double-pointed pieces of wood with stylized skeletal designs and small ivory spatulas with a stylized bear head at one end have no obvious function and may have been magicians' equipment. At Button Point on Bylot Island, the remains of six wooden masks, two drums, four carvings of human beings, twelve carvings of animals, and eight small double-pointed wood carvings were found within one square metre—perhaps the cache of a shaman. Other carvings may not have been related to magical activities. Naturalistic figures of birds, a small sculpture of two men arm-wrestling, and one of a father with a child on his shoulders may have been made simply for amusement. The general tone of the art, however, gives the impression of a concern with magic and witchcraft, and we may assume that these activities were of great importance in the lives of Dorset people.

By about A.D. 1000, the artists, magicians and hunters of the Dorset culture had developed a unique way of life, moulded to the Canadian Arctic by some 3000 years of isolated adaptation. Yet within a short period of time the Dorset culture disappeared, and it seems likely that all or most of the Dorset people became extinct. In most areas this probably occurred before A.D. 1000, despite one questionable radiocarbon date of 1350 for a Dorset site in the core area. Only along the east coast of Hudson Bay and in arctic Quebec, where dates as recent as 1400 occur, might Dorset people have survived to a later time.

We can only guess at the causes of this disappearance. The period around A.D. 1000 was one of rapidly warming climate, and this probably caused marked changes in sea-ice conditions and animal distributions throughout arctic Canada.

Some Dorset groups may have been unprepared for such changes in hunting conditions and starved. Shortly after A.D. 1000, a migration from the west brought the ancestors of the Inuit to arctic Canada. They may have killed some Dorset people and forced others into areas where they could not support themselves. If the Dorset were the Tunit of legend, and if we trust the legendary accounts, there must have been frequent, and at times friendly, contact between the two groups. Nevertheless, the legends generally end with the giant Tunit being driven from the country. This fate may be recounted archaeologically in the disappearance of the Dorset culture.

CHAPTER 5

Whalers in Skin Boats

Alaska (1000 B.C.–A.D. 1000)

Canst thou draw out Leviathan with an hook?
or his tongue with a cord
which thou lettest down?
Canst thou fill his skin with barbed irons?
or his head with fish spears?
Job 41: 1,7

At about the time that the book of Job was being written, ancestral Eskimos were beginning to discover that the great baleen whale could be drawn out of the Bering Sea, not with a hook but with a harpoon. The Bering Sea is one of the richest hunting grounds of the northern world. Resident populations of ringed and bearded seals are augmented by summer migrations of subarctic harbour and fur seals. Walrus haul out on the coasts and islands, beluga feed in the mouths of rivers, and whales funnel through the narrow gap of Bering Strait on their annual migration to and from summer feeding grounds in the arctic seas. Summer runs of salmon crowd most West Alaskan rivers, while caribou graze the coastal tundras and the nearby forests. It was probably along this coast, at some time during the first millennium B.C., that ancestral Eskimos began to develop an adaptation to seasonally frozen coasts. This adaptation, refined by several centuries of living around the Bering Sea, allowed their descendants of about one thousand years ago to move eastwards, bringing the Inuit way of life to arctic Canada.

The process by which this adaptation came about is far from clear. The Bering Sea coast of Alaska appears to have been only lightly occupied by people of the Arctic Small Tool tradition, and no ASTt sites are dated more recently than the late second millennium B.C. We do not know if the Alaskan

ASTt people became extinct at that time, if they moved northwards or to the interior, or if they contributed in some way to the new adaptation that began to appear in coastal regions. In view of the apparently small size and interior orientation of West Alaskan ASTt populations and the presence of maritime-oriented cultures, with probably larger populations, in the Aleutian Islands and along the coast of South Alaska, it seems reasonable to suggest that Bering Sea coastal adaptations were the result of influences, and perhaps people, moving northwards from the Pacific region.

The earliest evidence appeared at Cape Krusenstern, just north of Bering Strait, probably about 1000 B.C. This isolated find, consisting of a small village of five houses, yielded large projectile points of chipped flint among its few artifacts. Seal bones were found in the houses, and whale bones were scattered along the nearby beach; this circumstantial evidence for whaling activities led to the name Old Whaling culture. The way of life of these people and their relationship to other arctic peoples of the time remain a mystery. We might think of the Old Whaling culture as a short-lived attempt by a non-ASTt group, perhaps Aleuts or Eskimos or Indians, to adapt to the coast of the Bering Sea.

Slightly more is known about the next experiment, the Choris culture, which appeared in the area after about 1000 B.C. The Choris people lived in large, oval, semisubterranean houses, and hunted both seal and caribou. They had a chipped-stone industry, but it resembled that of the ASTt only in the excellence of the workmanship. Among its products are beautiful lanceolate spear points, which resemble those used by the Indians of central North America several millennia earlier. The few bone artifacts remind us of Aleutian or South Alaskan styles, and the linear-stamped pottery clearly was derived from that of nearby Siberian Neolithic peoples. The Choris people may have been South Alaskan Eskimos or Aleuts who moved northwards and changed the styles of their chipped-stone tools, or Indians who moved to the coast and adopted some aspects of Eskimo life, or Siberian immigrants who occupied an Alaskan beachhead for a few generations. We do not know where the Choris people came from or what their experience contributed to later adaptations to the Bering Sea coast.

We are on somewhat firmer ground with the Norton culture, which appeared in West Alaska after about 500 B.C. Here again, we find a curious blend of ASTt, South Alaskan and Siberian influences. The chipped-stone tools bear a vague resemblance to those of the ASTt, but there are none of the burins or microblades that are so characteristic of ASTt collections. Chipped-stone tools are to some extent replaced by tools of ground slate, a technique of stone-working that was developed in South Alaska. The bone tool industry and items such as labrets, which were worn as lip decorations, also remind us of South Alaska or the Aleutians. Norton pottery is well made and is decorated with check-stamping as is contemporaneous Siberian pottery.

Norton culture may be seen either as an adaptation by ASTt people who had learned much from the maritime hunters of South Alaska, or as an adaptation by South Alaskans who had moved north to the Bering Sea and learned from Siberians and from the remnants of a West Alaskan ASTt population. Whichever turns out to be the case, we can be reasonably certain of one thing: since we can trace cultural continuity from Norton times to the present day, the Norton people were almost certainly Eskimos. Norton is, in fact, the earliest archaeological culture that can be definitely ascribed to an Eskimo population. Although several of the cultures described—Choris, Old Whaling, ASTt, Dorset, the early cultures of South Alaska—may have been produced by Eskimos, we cannot be certain which were and which were not.

The Norton people occupied West Alaska between roughly 500 B.C. and A.D. 0, and later in some areas. To the north, Norton variants such as Ipiutak and Near-Ipiutak represent unique adaptations to the North Alaskan coast, and traces of Norton culture are found as far east as the Mackenzie River. As was mentioned in the previous chapter, we suspect some minimal contact and influence between the Norton culture and the contemporaneous Dorset culture of arctic Canada. Although no Norton sites are known from Siberia, the appearance of check-stamped pottery in Norton sites in Alaska suggests some contact with Siberian peoples. What we know archaeologically as the Norton culture probably includes a wide and variable range of adaptations to the western Arctic, which laid the basis for the later Eskimo way of life.

The best-known and probably the most significant development from a Norton culture base occurred on the eastern coast of the Chukchi Peninsula and on St. Lawrence Island in the Bering Sea. This was the Old Bering Sea culture, first recognized in 1926 by Diamond Jenness. In the Old Bering Sea culture, dated to the centuries immediately before and after A.D. 0, we first find the technology that allowed the Eskimos to adapt so efficiently to arctic maritime hunting. In the frozen and well-preserved ruins of houses on St. Lawrence Island and along the Siberian coast, we begin to find the technological gadgetry that was a feature of later Eskimo cultures—the elaboration of a technology more complex than that of any other

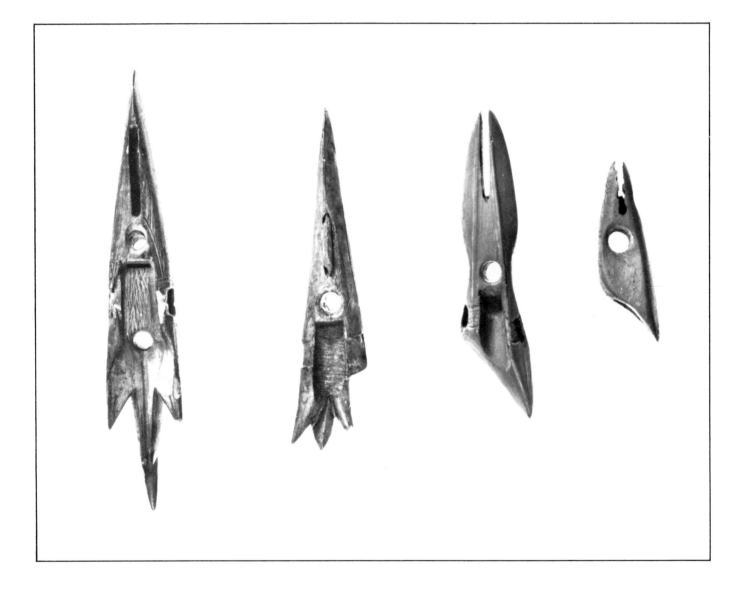

Plate 11. Style Changes in Inuit Harpoon Heads The Inuit gradually changed the styles of their harpoon heads, just as the earlier Dorset people had. From left to right are: harpoon heads from the Alaskan Old Bering Sea culture, 1500 to 2000 years old; from the North Alaskan Birnirk culture, 500 to 1000 years old; from the early Canadian Thule culture, about 1000 years old; and from late prehistoric Canadian Inuit culture. By following these style changes, we can trace the history of the Canadian Inuit back to their Alaskan origins.

pre-industrial culture, which allowed not only an economically efficient but also a comfortable way of life throughout arctic North America.

Perhaps the most significant invention of the time was the float-harpoon. With this sealskin float, inflated like a balloon and plugged with a mouthpiece of ivory or wood, the Old Bering Sea people were capable of hunting larger sea mammals from boats in open water. The line from the harpoon head no longer needed to be held in the hand but could be attached to a float. The float would not only tire a harpooned walrus or whale, but would also keep it afloat after death. At the same time, we find the first definite evidence for the use of skin-covered boats, both the one-man kayak and the larger umiak, an open boat, 8 to 10 metres long, that could be used to hunt whales as well as to move camp. Harpoons were thrown from these boats with wooden throwing boards, which increased the range of the weapons. Much of the harpoon gear was carved from ivory and was finely decorated, perhaps indicating ceremonial aspects of maritime hunting (see Colour Plate IV, page 60). Walrus and seals appear to have provided the basis for subsistence and probably were often hunted from boats. Although no whaling harpoon gear has been identified, whale bone and baleen are found in the villages, and whaling harpoon heads are known from the contemporaneous Near-Ipiatak culture of North Alaska. Winter sea-ice hunting was also important, as indicated by ice-creepers and the wooden snow goggles used to prevent snow-blindness. Small hand-pulled sleds had runners of wood and ivory. Although the Old Bering Sea people had dogs, there is no indication that they were used to pull sleds.

A new type of settlement pattern appeared at this time, perhaps related to the new hunting techniques or the consequent increase in the food supply. Villages were now larger and winter houses permanent. The houses were dug into the ground and roofed with skins and sod over supports of driftwood. They had sunken cold-trap entrance passages, were well insulated by the layer of sod on walls and roof, and were heated with pottery lamps that burned the oil of sea mammals. Within these warm, secure winter houses, we can imagine the Old Bering Sea people recounting the legends and practising the rituals that would form the basis of later Eskimo mythology and religion. Old Bering Sea art, preserved archaeologically in the form of carved ivory objects, has been compared with the art of the Northwest Coast Indians and the Chinese. Living between two worlds, with a technology that gave them an abundant and secure economy, they developed a way of life that was probably as rich as any other in the nonagricultural and nonindustrial world.

The descendants of the Old Bering Sea culture are known archaeologically as the Punuk culture, dating roughly between A.D. 500 and 1000. The Punuk people carried on the traditions of their ancestors, and built on them by adding new tools and weapons that provided a still more efficient economy. Some of these new elements may have come from Asia through trade and contact with Siberian peoples. Engraving tools and perhaps some knife blades were now made from small pieces of iron obtained through trade with Siberian Iron Age peoples. Armour made by sewing together slats of bone or ivory seems to be another Siberian introduction, appearing at the same time as the composite sinew-backed bow. These may have been introduced as weapons of war, but the new type of bow, which derived its strength from a cable of twisted sinew, would also have made possible more efficient hunting of land mammals and birds. Chipped-stone tools were almost entirely replaced by tools of ground slate, and there were other minor changes in artifact styles. The most impressive addition to Punuk technology, however, was the large harpoon head designed to hold the baleen whales that migrate each summer through Bering Strait. One bowhead whale, harpooned from a kayak or umiak and allowed to pull a series of floats or drags until it tired and could be lanced, would supply several tonnes of meat and blubber. Population appears to have increased during Punuk times. The Punuk people live in larger houses and larger villages, with richer garbage middens. The archaeological deposits on Punuk Island, the remnants of old houses and garbage, are piled to a depth of over six metres.

The influence of the Punuk culture spread far beyond the Bering Strait region, as far west as the mouth of the Kolyma River and as far east as the North Alaskan coast. At Point Barrow, Punuk influences are apparent in the contemporaneous Birnirk culture, a coastal hunting culture known from excavations there and at other similar locations. The North Alaskan coast is not as rich as the Bering Sea, but it does have one environmental feature that makes it an ideal location for hunting the largest of the arctic whales, the bowhead. Each spring the landfast ice of the Beaufort Sea splits into long, narrow leads, running parallel to the coast and ranging from a few hundred metres to a few kilometres from the shore. When the bowhead whales migrate along these leads to their summer feeding grounds, they can be harpooned from the ice edge or from boats launched into the narrow strips of water to which they are confined. In the nineteenth and early twentieth centuries, the North Alaskan Inuit harpooned several dozen of these whales each spring, and a few more during the autumn migration. This allowed the occupation of large permanent villages on every point of land that stretched out toward the ice-leads of the Beaufort Sea. Some of these villages were first established during the Birnirk period.

There is little evidence that early Birnirk people hunted whales, but about A.D. 1000 we do begin to find large amounts of whale bone and baleen in their middens, as well as whaling equipment like that of the Punuk culture. This change marks the beginning of what is known as the Thule culture, and the development of an adaptation that led to the second major wave of occupation to move across arctic Canada.

CHAPTER 6

The Second Wave

Thule Culture and the Inuit (A.D. 1000–1600)

*Whilest he was searching the countrie neere the shoare,
some of the people of the countrie shewed themselves,
leaping and dancing with straunge shrikes and cryes,
which gave no little admiration to our men.*
Dionyse Settle's account of Martin Frobisher's third voyage, 1578

During the centuries just before and after A.D. 1000, the northern hemisphere experienced a general warming trend. This was most marked in arctic regions where the tree line in central Canada advanced to about 100 kilometres north of its present position. Drift ice rarely reached as far south as Iceland and did not interfere with the Norse expansion to Greenland and eastern Canada. Between roughly 900 and 1200, normal arctic conditions were probably similar to what are now experienced during rare years of warm, ice-free summers and mild winters. These conditions have been cited as one reason for the Norse expansion throughout northern Europe and the North Atlantic, and they also may have contributed to the expansion of North Alaskan peoples. Arctic North America was invaded from two directions at that time: from the east by the Norse arriving in their wooden ships, and from the west by Alaskan Eskimos travelling in skin boats. These Alaskans brought with them a way of life that is known archaeologically as the Thule culture. They almost certainly spoke the *inuktitut* dialect of the Eskimo language, and we may refer to them and their descendants as Inuit.

The Thule culture, which appears to have had its origins in North Alaska, is named after Thule in northwestern Greenland where it was first identified. The similarity of Thule artifacts from Alaska to Greenland is remarkable, the most likely explanation being an extremely rapid movement of people from one end of

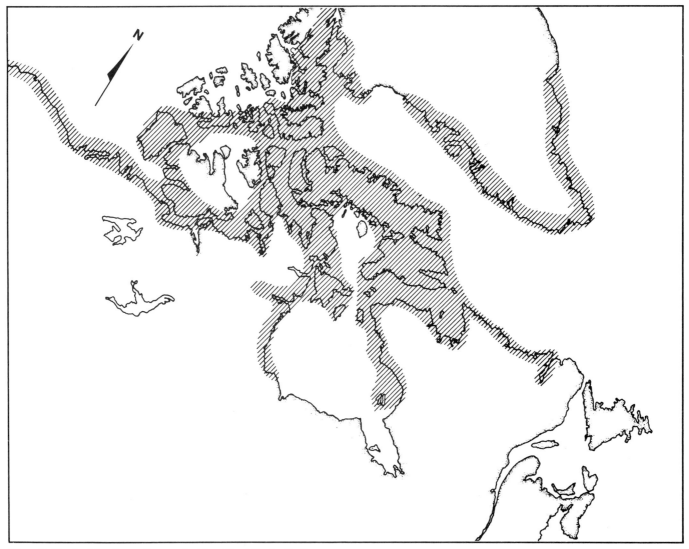

Map 6. Probable Area Occupied by the Thule Culture

arctic North America to the other. All across arctic Canada we find the remains of small Thule villages, some of which must represent the camps of people who took part in the original migration. Few of these villages have been excavated, and we can only guess how and why the Thule expansion took place.

The development of Thule culture seems to be closely connected to the development of techniques for hunting large whales, which were perfected during the first millennium A.D. by Bering Sea hunters. The resulting equipment and knowledge appear to have spread to North Alaska by about A.D. 1000, where it was probably put to use in hunting whales migrating close to shore along the narrow ice-leads. Some North Alaskan Thule people may have followed the migrating whales eastwards to their summer feeding grounds in the Beaufort Sea and in Amundsen Gulf, where the animals could be killed throughout the summer and not only during migration. Thule villages, usually containing much whale bone and baleen, are found scattered along the Amundsen Gulf coasts of the Canadian mainland and of Victoria and Banks islands. A few of these sites have produced harpoon heads of identical style to those used by the Alaskan ancestors of the Canadian Thule population. These early Thule harpoon heads turn up again in Thule villages on Cornwallis and Devon islands and in northwestern Greenland. By following the trail of this distinctive style of harpoon head, we may be able to trace the route of the original Thule expansion, which seems to follow the course used by large baleen whales during the early years of this millennium. At that time of reduced sea ice, the distributions of the western Arctic bowhead whale and the eastern Arctic Greenland whale—closely related animals both identified zoologically as *Balaena mysticetus*—may have been continuous throughout

Parry Channel. This would have provided Thule hunters with a familiar animal that could be hunted by the same methods from North Alaska, across the High Arctic, to Baffin Bay and Greenland.

Most early Thule villages were small, consisting of a few winter houses, and were probably occupied by fewer than fifty people. Camps of this size were probably the major social unit of the Thule Inuit, a loose grouping of related families who lived together in the winter village and hunted together during the summer. As in the camps of the later Inuit, the Thule people may have grouped around an older man whose experience and skill gave him the authority to advise the community on when and where to hunt and when the camp should be moved. The remainder of the group may have been made up of his sons and their families, the families of other male relatives, and occasionally the families of his daughters and of unrelated people.

The animal bones found in these villages suggest that food was abundant during the relatively mild and ice-free early Thule period. One small village of five houses, located in an area of Devon Island that is well over 100 kilometres north of the present limit of the bowhead whale, contained the bones of at least ten large whales. These whales would have averaged between 10 and 20 metres long, and each would have yielded several tonnes of meat and blubber. This resource allowed a relatively sedentary existence, and probably meant that a relatively high proportion of children survived to rapidly increase the Thule population. Most villages appear to have been occupied for only a few years, probably less than a generation. We can imagine villages splitting up because of murders or less violent disagreements, or upon the death of a father when

Plate 12. Scenes from Thule Life
An insight into Thule life can be
gained from the small incised pictures
on Thule artifacts. These scenes are
from an ivory bow-drill found near
Arctic Bay. Top: summer tents, in
front of which men appear to be
fighting with bows and spears.
Centre: kayakers encounter a
swimming caribou and, above, men
paddle two umiaks. Bottom: whalers
harpoon a spouting whale, while bear
skins dry in front of a tent camp.

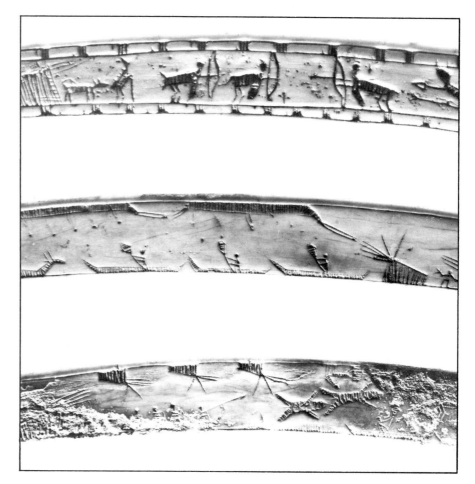

Plate 13. Thule Land-Hunting Equipment The Thule people brought with them an elaborate technology for hunting land mammals and for fishing in interior rivers and lakes. The fishing gear on the upper left includes: a composite bone-and-wood fish-hook with braided sinew line, a large copper gaff hook, a barb from a fish spear, a fish-shaped lure used to attract fish to the spear, and a double-pointed gorge used with a set-line. At upper right are: two barbed arrowheads, an ivory pin for closing the wound of a slain animal, and the prong of a bird spear. At bottom, from right to left, are: the bone tip of a composite bow, a sinew-twister for tightening the sinew cable that gave the bow its power, a centre prong for a bird spear, and three bone blocks for a bolas, which when tied together were thrown at low-flying birds.

two brothers thought it best to each take their people to a new area. An entire camp could probably pack all of their children, dogs and equipment into one or two umiaks, which would be rowed by the women while the men travelled in their hunting kayaks. A new winter village could be built in a few days at any place where a whale was killed or where seals or walrus could provide winter food. Under such conditions, a small mobile population could conceivably spread from Alaska to Greenland within a few generations.

The hunting technology of the Thule people was firmly rooted in that of their Alaskan ancestors. For hunting at sea they used the kayak and the umiak. The amount of whale bone and baleen in early Thule villages indicates that the old Punuk whaling harpoon and float was used to kill many of the slow-moving baleen whales that spend the summer in arctic feeding grounds. Float harpoons could also be thrown from the ice edge or from kayaks to capture smaller whales, seals and walrus. The harpoon was adapted for winter hunting of ringed and bearded seals at breathing holes, and here Inuit inventiveness resulted in the development of several specialized tools: probes to detect the shape of the breathing hole, indicators to show when a seal arrived at the hole, stools for the sealer to sit on, ice-creepers to prevent him from slipping, snow goggles to prevent snow-blindness, plugs to close the seal's wounds and preserve its blood, and special toggles for pulling the animal home across the ice. Winter hunting was also made easier by the use of dogsleds, which seem to have originated with the early Thule people. These are represented archaeologically by fragments of the komatik type of sled, bone sled shoes drilled and pinned to the runners to prevent damage, specialized harness toggles and trace buckles, and the handles of dog whips.

Plate 14. A Thule Winter House
This house, like others in the same 500-year-old Devon Island village, has the skull of a bowhead whale placed above the entrance. The house is built of stone slabs, boulders and sod.

Plate 15. A Thule Winter House after Excavation   The collapsed roof has been cleared from this house, revealing a well-preserved living area. The house was dug into the ground and surrounded by walls of piled boulders. At the front is a sunken entrance tunnel leading to a flagstone floor with a cooking area in each corner. At the rear is a raised sleeping platform, also covered with flagstones, and beneath this are lockers for storing equipment.

Colour Plate V. The Remains of a Thule Village The winter villages of the Thule people range in size from a single house to over thirty houses. When the villages were abandoned, the whalebone roof supports of the houses collapsed over the stone walls and floors, leaving a mound of rubble. The decaying refuse in the houses provides nutrients that support a luxuriant plant growth, even in the most barren areas of the High Arctic.

Thule hunters also depended on land animals for clothing and food. Caribou and musk-oxen were shot with a sinew-backed bow or were killed with spears thrown from kayaks. Waterfowl were killed with blunt arrows, special bird spears with three side-prongs, or the bolas—a group of bone weights tied together with thongs and flung at low-flying birds. Fish were speared with tridents or caught with gorges and jigging-hooks. Animals were butchered with slate-bladed knives, and cooked in containers that were originally made of pottery but later of soapstone.

Thule home life can be partially reconstructed from the frozen remains of their winter houses. These followed the old Alaskan pattern but were built of stones and whale bones rather than of logs. A Thule winter house is usually an irregular oval in outline, measuring roughly five metres from side to side. At the front is an entrance tunnel built of stone slabs or boulders, and usually sloping downwards to form a cold-trap that prevents cold air from entering the house. The interior of the house is divided into two sections. In the front is a floor area paved with flagstones and with one or two cooking areas in the corners. At the back, raised about 20 centimetres above the floor, is a flagstone platform on which the family members slept side by side, with their feet toward the back wall. Storage lockers are located beneath the sleeping platform, which is covered with a springy mattress made of baleen cut into strips and tied together in loops. This was probably covered with skins and furnished with blankets of caribou skin, making a very comfortable bed. The roof of the house is dome-shaped, held up by rafters of whale jaws and ribs set in the stones of the outer wall and tied together at the top. This frame was covered with skins, then with a thick layer of turf and moss, and

Colour Plate VI. Thule Sea-Hunting Equipment Sea mammals provided the basic subsistence for most Thule people. The large artifact on the left is a harpoon head used in hunting the large bowhead whale; next to it are two smaller harpoon heads and a lance head with slate blade. Beneath the latter are a nozzle and plug from a sealskin float, which was attached to a harpoon line for hunting in open water; a trace buckle from a dogsled harness; and an ivory toggle used to drag seals across the ice. At lower left is a set of snow goggles, which were worn to prevent snow-blindness while ice-hunting.

finally probably thickly banked with snow. Such a house must have been almost perfectly insulated and probably required a ventilation hole in the roof. The house was heated with blubber lamps.

The long winter night of the High Arctic must have passed pleasantly in the lamplight and warmth of the Thule house. Food and fuel for the lamps were obtained from caches made during the previous summer; most villages were surrounded by such caches, covered with heavy boulders to protect them from dogs, foxes and bears. Winter was probably the season for visits and gossip, for telling stories of last summer's whale hunts and of ancestral days in the towns of Alaska. It was the season for song contests and dances (indicated archaeologically by drum fragments) and for religious ceremonies. The unique religion and mythology of the historic Inuit must have had their origins in the villages of the Thule people. Winter was also a time for carving ivory harpoon heads and other tools, for decorating the combs and needle cases of the women with incised camp or hunting scenes, and for making toys for the children. Toy bows, toy cooking pots, wooden dolls, and spinning-tops made from the discs of whale vertebrae are found in all Thule villages. Games that left archaeological traces include *ajegaq*, which involved tossing a bone drilled with holes into the air and catching it on a pin, and a hand game that awarded points for throwing small carved birds or bird-women figures so that they landed on their flat bases. In northwestern Greenland, Thule carvers made replicas of chessmen used by the Norse settlers of southwestern Greenland, and some may even have learnt to play chess. To the archaeologist, spending his nights alone on the gravel floor of a windblown tent, the excavation of a Thule winter house is an

Plate 16. Thule Fox Trap This stone structure, built about 400 years ago on southern Ellesmere Island, is one of 50 fox traps clustered around one village. The fox jumped through the small entrance at the top of the vaulted structure in order to get the bait but was unable to jump out again.

exercise in envy. Having felt only pity in digging up the remains of an Independence I camp, or the fearful awareness of an alien civilization on the site of a Dorset village, the archaeologist can only compare his life unfavourably with that of the Thule man who built a house from the bones and skins of animals he had killed with his own hands, a house where he could spend the dark months of winter warm and secure with his wife and children.

In the brightening days of late winter, the men spent their days hunting seals at breathing holes, and then on the ice or at the ice edge. Snow probes and snow knives are common archaeological finds, indicating that some Thule people probably lived in domed snowhouses on the sea ice during this season, developing the winter lifestyle that would later be adopted by the historic Inuit. Winter houses must have become uninhabitable when the ground thawed and water filled the floor areas. Early summer probably saw a move to skin tents pitched on the beach. From these camps the men could hunt sea mammals from their kayaks, or could move inland to take advantage of the fish runs and caribou migrations of the inland regions.

Summer hunting involved the building of fish weirs, boulder dams behind which the fish could be trapped and speared. Thule hunters also built lines of piled stones to serve as drive-fences, which directed caribou toward hunters armed with bows, or toward water crossings where they could be speared from kayaks. Conical tower-traps and small box-traps with sliding doors were built in large numbers to catch the arctic fox. In southern Ellesmere Island, Thule people built huge sliding-door traps to capture bears.

The dead were buried in boulder-covered cairns, which in some areas were grouped to form large cemeteries. Lines of

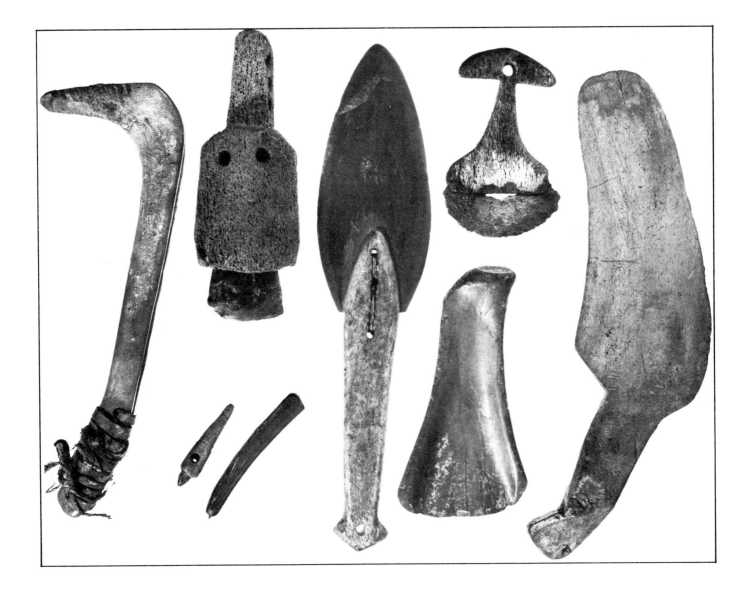

Plate 17. Thule Technology The technology of the Thule people made use of a great variety of materials. The artifacts illustrated here include, clockwise from the left: an antler adze handle; a whalebone adze head with polished stone blade; a flensing knife with a ground-slate blade; an ulu with a blade made of iron, either imported or meteoric; a whalebone snow knife, used to cut blocks for building snowhouses; a bone scraper used in preparing hides; an ivory engraving tool with a small iron point; and a drill bit with a ground-stone point.

"jumping stones" were constructed near villages as part of a game or trial of strength. The boulder dams, drive-fences, tent rings, traps, meat caches and cairns that were constructed by Thule builders mark most landscapes of arctic Canada. Thule people seem to have enjoyed moving large boulders, and some of the rocks they lifted are almost impossibly heavy. The Thule occupation of arctic Canada has been called a geological event, second only to the glaciers of the last Ice Age in modifying the arctic landscape.

Spring travel by sled and summer travel by boat probably formed a loose but widespread link between communities throughout the Thule world. New inventions and new styles of artifacts spread rapidly throughout the Arctic from Greenland to Alaska. The Thule people were also in contact with the non-Inuit world. Every excavated Thule village has produced some evidence of the use of iron, usually in small chunks that were used as tips for harpoon heads or as blades for knives and engraving tools. Some of this iron was of meteoric origin, but most was probably passed from village to village as trade items originating either in Siberia or in the Norse colonies in Greenland. In return, the furs of fox and bear the Thule Inuit trapped, the ivory tusks of narwhal and walrus they killed, and perhaps the gyrfalcons they captured may have reached the courts of Europe and China. Early contact between Thule people and the Greenlandic Norse probably occurred between isolated hunting or trading parties. After about 1300, however, Inuit began to move southwards along the coast of Greenland where, if we can trust vague Norse accounts and Inuit legends, they may have had a hand in the extinction of the Norse colonies. In the eastern Arctic, the Thule people met, fought and traded with European adventurers such as Martin Frobisher and John Davis.

Plate 18. First Contact with Europeans John White painted this encounter between Martin Frobisher's men and the Thule Inuit of Baffin Island.

After about 1200, the climate of arctic Canada began to cool. This trend, resulting in longer winters and more extensive sea ice, may have caused the starvation and extinction of many Thule groups. Others must have adapted to the change by learning to use other resources. During the period from roughly 1200 to 1600 local Thule populations responded to the changed conditions of each area. On Victoria Island in the Central Arctic, we find Thule people hunting caribou and fishing during the summer, probably sealing at breathing holes during the winter, and learning to do without the whales that their ancestors hunted in the open water of Amundsen Gulf. Adaptations of this sort made possible the occupation of most of arctic Canada, including the nonwhaling areas of the Central Arctic and the coasts of Hudson Bay.

During the original migration or the later period of adjustment and expansion, local Thule groups may have encountered some of their predecessors, the people of the Dorset culture. Archaeological evidence of such contact is scarce. A few Thule winter houses contain Dorset artifacts, which may have been left by a remnant Dorset population that had learnt to build houses in the new style. On the other hand, many of these cases are probably mistakes of archaeological interpretation, such as might result from a Thule house being roofed with sods dug from a Dorset midden. The remaining evidence for contact is purely circumstantial. Thule people built domed snowhouses, for example, and we suspect that they learned the technique from their Dorset predecessors. Canadian Thule people soon replaced their pottery containers and lamps with ones carved from soapstone; soapstone vessels had been used for centuries by Dorset people, but the Thule vessels were made in completely different styles. Perhaps the most convincing evidence of contact is in the form of a harpoon head that was popular among eastern Arctic Thule and historic Inuit, and which resembles Dorset forms more closely than any Thule prototype. If we identify the legendary Tunit with the Dorset people, we can assume that contact between the two groups occurred often, and may occasionally have been peaceful or even friendly. Eventually, however, the Dorset way of life disappeared, probably contributing in only a minor way to the Thule Inuit adaptation to arctic Canada. The archaeological evidence agrees with that of legend: the Dorsets were driven away, probably by being displaced from the best hunting areas by the Thule people, who outnumbered them, were armed with superior weapons, and perhaps had a heritage of warfare that they brought with them from Alaska. The historic Inuit are the descendants of these invaders of about a thousand years ago.

CHAPTER 7

The Little Ice Age

The Development of Inuit Cultures
(A.D. 1600–1850)

It was the first time I saw them,
Munching the flowers of the plain—
Great black giant beasts
Far from any village
In the lands of our happy summer hunting.
Igjugarjuk's song of the musk-oxen, Barren Grounds, 1922

Both the genetic and cultural heritage of the Inuit is firmly based in that of the Thule people, a population and a way of life that originated in Alaska and was transferred to arctic Canada by a rapid expansion of population about A.D. 1000. It is this recent population expansion and migration that accounts for the genetic uniformity of modern Inuit and for the similarity of all *inuktitut* dialects spoken between Greenland and the Bering Strait. Yet by the eighteenth and nineteenth centuries, when Europeans began to penetrate arctic Canada and describe the people they met, their descriptions were not of a uniform maritime-oriented culture but of a series of peoples whose ways of life differed greatly from one area to another. Most of these differences had developed since the breakup, which began about 1200, of the originally uniform span of the Thule culture. Many of the recent changes in Inuit culture can be seen as the result of local responses to changing environmental conditions and as part of a general adaptation to the cooling climate of the past several centuries.

Evidence from glaciology and palaeobotany combined with European historical records indicates that arctic climates began to cool by about 1200, reaching a cold peak known as the Little Ice Age between roughly 1600 and 1850. Glaciers advanced on the islands of the eastern Arctic, the tree line retreated to its present position, sea ice increased in area and

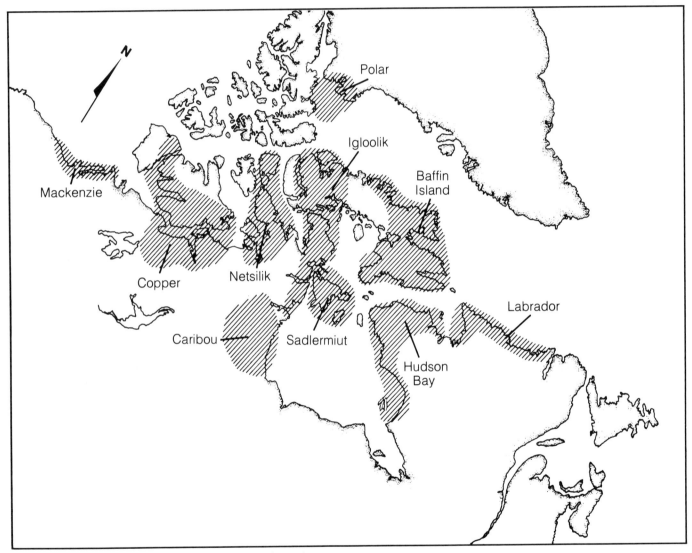

Map 7. Historic Inuit Occupations of Arctic Canada

duration in the North Atlantic and probably throughout the Arctic, and the populations and ranges of many animal species probably changed markedly. Perhaps the most significant change was the disappearance of bowhead and Greenland whales from many areas, because the increased extent and duration of the sea ice prevented them from reaching their summer feeding grounds. These conditions may also have limited the range and number of smaller whales, walrus and migratory seals. The only important species that may have increased in number and range was the small ringed seal, which lives and breeds beneath winter ice. This animal, as well as the caribou and musk-ox of the interior, became the mainstay of life for Inuit populations living in areas where their Thule ancestors had hunted whales from open boats.

The Thule response to the Little Ice Age resulted in a series of local cultures, each adapted to the resources of a specific area. Different geographical regions were inhabited by a series of small bands named after local areas, each having a slightly different dialect and way of life. The degree of difference between neighbouring groups was small but increased with the distance between groups.

Anthropologists have generally clustered these local groups into "tribes," such as Labrador Eskimo or Mackenzie Eskimo, which represent fairly uniform regional adaptations. Such "tribal" grouping was not especially significant to the Inuit, and it should be realized that the definitions and names of these groups are artificial and arbitrary. The best way to summarize the cultures of these groups is in terms of the adaptations people made to the resources of nine geographical regions: Labrador, Arctic Quebec, Southern Baffin Island, Northern Baffin Island and Foxe Basin, Southampton Island,

Plate 19. Snowhouse Village
During the Little Ice Age, many Inuit groups abandoned the permanent winter houses occupied by their Thule ancestors and began to spend the winters in large snowhouse villages. From these villages they hunted seals at breathing holes in the winter ice.

Western Hudson Bay and the Barren Grounds, Central Arctic Coast, Mackenzie Delta and the High Arctic.

The earliest-known Inuit occupation of Labrador dates from about 1500, when Thule people began to cross Hudson Strait and spread down the coast as far as Hamilton Inlet. The annual migrations of Greenland whales and harp seals along this coast, together with resident populations of ringed seals and walrus, allowed an easy extension of the Thule way of life to the region. The Inuit of Labrador soon came into contact with European whalers and fishermen, who began to exploit the southern coast about the same time. During the late sixteenth and early seventeenth centuries, the Inuit began to make voyages to the Strait of Belle Isle area to trade and to plunder the European shore stations. They soon provided themselves with whaling boats and many other European items, and their attacks may have contributed to the abandonment of the Basque whale fishery in southern Labrador.

A change in Labrador Inuit life seems to have occurred about 1700. This is marked archaeologically by the disappearance of the Thule style of winter house and its replacement by the large rectangular house designed to hold several families. Dating from about the same time, there was a sharp decrease in the amount of baleen found in the houses. It has been argued that whaling may have become less important at this time, perhaps because of changed ice conditions or because European whaling had reduced the whale population. The move to multifamily houses may have been connected with this and with a new need for cooperation in hunting seals and sharing winter food, or perhaps to economic changes associated with European trade. A similar change to large rectangular houses occurred among the Inuit of southwestern Greenland at about the same time, and possibly for the same reasons. Despite this change the Labrador Inuit still hunted whales in the 1770s, when Moravian missionaries established their stations along the northern coast. Labrador was probably less affected by the Little Ice Age than most arctic areas, and the Inuit were therefore able to preserve most aspects of the Thule way of life into historic times.

Little is known of the archaeology of Inuit occupations along the southern coast of Hudson Strait and the eastern coast of Hudson Bay. We can only assume that the history of the area was similar to that of Labrador.

Thule people occupied southern and eastern Baffin Island by at least 1200, probably spreading down the coast from the north. Here again, the presence of whales and other sea mammals in the open waters of Baffin Bay and Hudson Strait allowed the Thule people to follow their preferred way of life. The people Martin Frobisher met in 1576-78 were Thule Inuit, and the iron-tipped arrow that struck Frobisher was a Thule arrow. Contact with European mariners, traders and pirates likely continued sporadically from that time to the coming of the American and Scottish whalers who frequented Baffin Bay during the nineteenth century. This contact probably influenced the development of local cultures as much as did the Little Ice Age, which, as in Labrador, probably caused little change in the hunting conditions in Baffin Bay and Hudson Strait. Also as in Labrador, eighteenth-century Inuit moved from small, single-family houses to large, multifamily structures; but on Baffin Island these houses were used only during the early winter, and were formed by joining several individual houses to a common entrance passage. In most other characteristics the Thule way of life prevailed until the middle of the nineteenth century, when the local culture began to change rapidly through involvement in European whaling and trading.

Approaching the Central Arctic, we begin to encounter historic Inuit groups whose way of life was markedly different from that of their Thule ancestors. Northern Baffin Island and the coasts of the Melville Peninsula were occupied historically by groups that are classified as Iglulingmiut, the people of the Igloolik area. This area was originally settled by Thule people as early as 1200, and the Thule immigrants soon adapted their economy to the resources of walrus and caribou, which are still features of the region. It was probably at some time during the Little Ice Age that local Thule people stopped living in permanent winter houses and substituted skin-covered autumn houses, which were occupied only during the early winter. After the midwinter darkness, when stable sea ice had formed, people moved onto the ice and passed the remainder of the winter in snowhouse villages. Summers were spent hunting on the coast from the ice edge or from kayaks, and river fishing and caribou hunting in the interior. The large skin boat, the umiak, was dropped from the local technology, probably because the absence of whales and the short summer period of open water made it unnecessary. The Iglulingmiut were relatively isolated from European penetration of the Arctic. Aside from infrequent contact with explorers and a small amount of European trade goods that reached them from the south, they remained independent of the European fur trade until the late nineteenth century.

Southampton Island in northwestern Hudson Bay, as well as nearby Coats and Walrus islands, was inhabited by a group known to their neighbours as Sadlermiut. We know little about them, aside from brief descriptions by nineteenth-century

Colour Plate VII. Thule Art

Whereas the art of the Dorset people appears to have been primarily magical in character, the Thule Inuit applied their talents to decorating equipment used in everyday life, and to making toys. This collection includes, clockwise from upper left: an ivory pendant; a woman's comb; a needle case; an anchor-shaped thimble holder; an ivory pin of unknown use; a toy snow knife, bucket and dogsled harness toggle; an ivory chain; a pendant; a bird-woman carving; a bird carving; a lamp trimmer; and a wooden doll.

whalers and the vague memories of neighbouring Inuit. The Sadlermiut became extinct in 1900 as a result of an epidemic disease introduced by the crew of a Scottish whaling ship, the *Active*. There has been much speculation about the Sadlermiut, especially about the possibility that they were a remnant Dorset population. This speculation is based on only two clues: the Sadlermiut used chipped-stone tools instead of the ground-slate tools used by other Thule peoples, and the claim by neighbouring groups that the Sadlermiut spoke a strange dialect. On the other hand, their houses and most of their artifacts are firmly based in a Thule ancestry, indicating that the Sadlermiut were probably Inuit. Only further archaeological work will reveal the history of this enigmatic group. After the extinction of the Sadlermiut, the rich hunting areas of Southampton Island were occupied by people who came from the northwestern coast of Hudson Bay.

In the nineteenth century, the Barren Grounds west of Hudson Bay were occupied by Inuit who depended almost entirely on fish and caribou and who rarely, if ever, visited the coast to hunt seals. To early twentieth-century anthropologists the inland Caribou Eskimos, who lacked many of the elements of a maritime adaptation, were seen as remnants of an extremely primitive culture that had not yet learnt to adapt to the arctic coast. However, recent archaeological work has shown that the history of these people was quite different.

Thule villages spread down the western coast of Hudson Bay as far as Rankin Inlet by about 1200, and some of these people must have soon discovered the immense herds of caribou that migrated annually from the tree line to summer calving grounds around Chesterfield Inlet. They probably could not make much use of this resource, however, as most

Colour Plate VIII. Late-Prehistoric Inuit Artifacts By the nineteenth century the Inuit had abandoned or simplified many elements of Thule technology, changed the styles of their artifacts, and added some new elements and materials. This collection comes from the Coppermine area and includes, clockwise from upper left: a fish-hook with bone body and native copper hook, an arrowhead with copper blade, an ulu with copper blade, a native copper knife blade, a burin with an iron blade, a bone toggle, a marline-spike, a sinew-twister used to adjust the sinew cable of a bow, and a sealing harpoon head with copper blade.

of the Barren Grounds were occupied by ancestral Chipewyan Indians. When Samuel Hearne wandered through the area in the 1770s with Chipewyan companions, he encountered no Inuit south of Bloody Falls on the Coppermine River. In the eighteenth century the Inuit of the western coast of Hudson Bay became involved with the Hudson's Bay Company, whose trading sloops made annual voyages northwards from Churchill. During the nineteenth century this trade was supplemented by contact with American and Scottish whalers, who established shore stations in Roe's Welcome Sound. By the middle of the nineteenth century, the Inuit of the region were well supplied with traps, rifles and many other European goods. Meanwhile, the Indian occupation of the Barren Grounds had come to an end, largely as a result of the smallpox epidemics of the 1780s, which decimated the Chipewyan. With guns and ammunition making caribou hunting much more efficient, and with steel traps ensuring an adequate supply of furs to be traded for European goods, Inuit groups abandoned the coasts and moved into the interior. By the early twentieth century, they had developed a way of life so unusual that several anthropologists considered it an isolated continuation of the most ancient Eskimo pattern.

On the Central Arctic Coast, between Pelly Bay and Dolphin and Union Strait, lived Inuit who resembled the Caribou Eskimo in that they had dropped the maritime hunting technology of their ancestors. However, unlike the Caribou Eskimo, they spent the winter sealing on the sea ice. The more easterly of these groups have usually been classified as the Netsilingmiut, the seal people. The westerly inhabitants of the Coronation Gulf region have been called the Copper Eskimos because many of their tools are made of native copper. Thule penetration of this area

Plate 20. Inuit Summer Life   During the past few centuries, many Inuit groups gave up the summer coastal hunting practised by their Thule forbears. Instead, they spent the summer months in the interior hunting caribou and musk-oxen and fishing in the rivers and lakes.

probably occurred between 1200 and 1500 and involved an immediate change in the Thule way of life, since the shallow gulfs and channels of the Central Arctic did not support populations of whales or walrus. These Thule immigrants concentrated on hunting caribou, fishing, and learning to hunt ringed seals at their breathing holes in the winter ice. Nevertheless, they followed their ancestral pattern of spending at least part of the winter in permanent houses built of stones, sod and driftwood; Samuel Hearne, in 1771, described two such structures on the Coppermine River at Bloody Falls. The Thule immigrants soon discovered the local deposits of native copper and soapstone, which they used to make their tools and containers. The soapstone lamps and pots made in this region were traded as far west as North Alaska.

The Thule pattern of life began to break down during the Little Ice Age, and people began to live in dwellings no more permanent than the skin tent and the domed snowhouse. It was probably at this time that the western groups abandoned open water hunting and began using their kayaks only for spearing caribou at lake and river crossings. Throughout this area, summer and autumn were spent wandering about the interior in small bands, fishing and hunting caribou and musk-oxen. In early winter these bands grouped at coastal locations, and when the ice was stable they moved to snowhouse villages of approximately a hundred people, becoming totally dependent upon the seals that could be harpooned at breathing holes. As with the Caribou Eskimos, these people abandoned the umiak, the float harpoon and many other elements of Thule technology. In comparison with that of their Thule ancestors, the technology of the historic Inuit of the Central Arctic appears simple and crude, adapted to the nomadic life that was forced on them by the changing environment. Some of these groups came into contact with European explorers and traders during the early twentieth century, and anthropologists of the time considered their way of life to be a primitive relic of an ancient cultural pattern.

The coast of the Beaufort Sea between Dolphin and Union Strait and Cape Bathurst is a poor hunting area and does not appear to have been occupied after the early Thule period. This unoccupied stretch of 500 kilometres served to isolate the Inuit of arctic Canada from the richer and more populous regions to the west. The Inuit classified as Mackenzie Eskimos lived along the coast between Cape Bathurst and Barter Island and were essentially Alaskans in their way of life. Those living along the outer headlands used umiaks to hunt the occasional bowhead whale, whereas those in the Mackenzie Delta region depended on fish and beluga. They spent the winters in large houses built of driftwood, used pottery lamps and containers, wore labrets in their lips and cheeks, travelled by umiak, and were in close contact with the North Alaskan Inuit to the west.

The archaeology of this area is little known. Excavations at the village of Kittigazuit, located at the mouth of the East Channel of the Mackenzie River, indicate that the ancestors of the Kittegaryumiut have lived in the area following the same rich beluga-hunting economy for at least the past 500 years. Kittigazuit was a summer beluga-hunting camp, occupied by up to a thousand people, and was the largest Inuit community between Bering Strait and Greenland. The ancestors of the Kittegaryumiut may have been Thule people who moved to the area about a thousand years ago, but it is equally likely that they came to the Mackenzie Delta at an earlier, pre-Thule period. Only future archaeological work will reveal the history of this large segment of the Canadian Inuit population.

When Europeans began to penetrate the eastern High Arctic in the nineteenth century, they found the area uninhabited except for some Greenland Inuit who made occasional hunting trips to Ellesmere Island. Archaeology shows that the area had once been occupied by Thule people and their descendants, perhaps as recently as the seventeenth century. These people may have been related to the Polar Eskimos of northwestern Greenland, and they probably occupied the Canadian High Arctic until the increased extent and duration of sea ice in the eighteenth century made the area uninhabitable. The High Arctic did not offer the alternative resources that enabled the Inuit of the Central Arctic to adapt to the Little Ice Age, and local groups must have either starved or moved to join their relatives clustered around the bird cliffs and open water areas of northwestern Greenland. The northern islands of the Canadian arctic archipelago were abandoned to the birds and animals, whose ancestors had seen the first humans occupy the area some 4000 years earlier.

Epilogue

It has long been fashionable to regard the Inuit of arctic Canada as a very "primitive" people. Living in perhaps the most demanding environment ever occupied by the human race, they are seen as a survival of an ancient way of life that was prevented by its harsh environment from achieving the social and cultural complexities that characterize "advanced" societies.

Archaeology shows this view to be false. The ancestors of the Inuit moved to arctic Canada within only the last thousand years, bringing with them a culture as rich and complex as that of any other nonagricultural or nonindustrial people. They came to arctic Canada at a time when the environment allowed them to maintain that way of life in their new home. Only during the last few centuries, when the climatic deterioration of the Little Ice Age no longer allowed that way of life to survive, did they develop the ingenious and unique adaptations that were described by early European explorers.

Inuit culture may be better understood by not looking on it as a relic of an archaic and primitive way of life. Rather, it should be seen as the result of a recent attempt to maintain the basic elements of a rich and sophisticated culture that could no longer be supported by the deteriorating arctic environment of the past three hundred years.

The traces of past events mark most arctic landscapes. On full view, rather than hidden by vegetation as in more southern latitudes, these traces give the arctic traveller a sense of history, of the importance of the past in shaping the present. The rock cairns and beacons of the nineteenth-century European explorers still stand on many prominent hills and headlands. Beaches are covered with the boulder tent rings, the animal bones and the tools lost or discarded by Inuit occupants over the past few centuries. Every few hours, the coastal traveller encounters the sod and whalebone mounds of a Thule winter village, and the boulder structures raised by Thule builders are scattered over the countryside. At higher elevations are the less obvious remains of rectangular Dorset houses, the circular tent rings of the Pre-Dorset period, and the isolated hearths built by the Independence I people some 4000 years ago. On hilltops one finds the spearheads left by early Indian hunters who followed the caribou northwards into the early postglacial Barren Grounds. The gravel bars of the unglaciated Old Crow Flats yield rare tools made by the first people to occupy North America, Palaeolithic hunters of elephants and horses on the tundras of the last Ice Age.

It is only by interpreting these remains of the past that we can learn the history of the Inuit and of other arctic peoples. At present we have only traced the outlines of this history, and are uncertain about many of our interpretations. We must fill in this history and check our interpretations through more extensive and more detailed archaeological excavation.

Unfortunately, the very prominence of archaeological sites in the Arctic makes them vulnerable to destruction through commercial activity or idle curiosity. Oil-exploration crews destroy the beacons of the Franklin Search Expeditions in the vain hope of finding souvenirs. Inuit people dig up local sites for artifacts that can be sold to visitors, and search Thule winter houses for the aged whalebone that can be used for carving. Each site is a unique piece of the puzzle of arctic history, and the destruction of any site means an opportunity lost.

Most destruction is not done maliciously, but because

Plate 21. The Ruins of a Nineteenth Century Explorer's Camp
The ruins of Northumberland House and the monument in memory of Sir John Franklin mark the headquarters of the Franklin Search Expeditions on Beechey Island.

people do not realize the value of an old site when it is carefully excavated and interpreted by a trained archaeologist. This book ends with a plea to northern residents and travellers to respect their history, and to leave the traces of the past undisturbed until they can be used to piece together that history. If we all cooperate in this, we should be able in a few years time to write a much better history of arctic Canada.

Glossary

Arctic Small Tool tradition   The name given by archaeologists to the remains left by the earliest peoples to occupy most northern arctic regions. The flint tools made by these people are characteristically very small and are similar in style to those made by Siberian peoples of about the same time. The Denbigh culture of Alaska and the Canadian Independence, Pre-Dorset and Dorset cultures all belong within this tradition.

Baleen   Sheets of this fibrous, plastic-like material are found in the mouths of several species of large whale and serve to strain from the sea water the small crustaceans that the whales eat. This useful material is the "whalebone" sought by nineteenth-century European whalers.

Blubber lamp   A lamp, usually made of pottery or stone, which burns oil rendered from the fat of sea mammals. The smokeless flame of the blubber lamp can be used to light and heat a well-insulated winter house. Its invention made possible the use of the snowhouse, which could not be heated with a smoking, open fire.

Bolas   A weapon, consisting of several bone weights tied together by strings, used for capturing low-flying ducks or geese. When thrown, the weights fan out to form a whirling wheel in which the birds become entangled.

Bow-drill   An efficient type of drill consisting of a spindle, which carries the bit, and a small bow. A loop of the bowstring is wound around the spindle, which is then rapidly turned by moving the bow back and forth.

Burin   A flint tool used for cutting grooves in bone or ivory as a first step in removing strips from which tools or weapons could be made. Arctic Small Tool tradition burins are made in a specific style, from thin, mitten-shaped flakes of stone. Tiny spalls were removed from one corner of these in order to form a chisel-like cutting edge.

Burin-like tool   The Dorset people, as well as the contemporaneous Norton people in Alaska, formed the edges of their grooving-tools by grinding the flint, rather than by striking off spalls to form true burins.

Composite bow   The hardwoods, which most peoples have used to make strong bows, were not available to Eskimos. Consequently, the Eskimo bow is generally made of several materials (antler, musk-ox horn, driftwood) lashed together. The bow's strength comes from a cable of twisted sinew lashed to the back of the bow. The Eskimo bow is generally of the Asiatic double-curve type (recurved), rather than the single-curve type used by most American Indians and early Europeans.

Deadfall   A type of trap that uses a falling weight to capture small animals; in the Arctic, most of these traps are built of stones.

Drive-fence   Caribou and other herd animals can be driven towards a concealed hunter. At locations where this type of hunting was practised regularly, arctic hunters built lines of rock piles to prevent the caribou from straying from the desired direction. The rock piles were sometimes built to resemble humans; these were called *inuksuit*.

Eskimo A European word that was first used in the sixteenth century to designate a group of Algonkian Indians who lived on the north shore of the Gulf of St. Lawrence. The name may be derived from the Algonkian word meaning "eaters of raw meat," or from the French word meaning "the excommunicated." By the eighteenth century it was applied to the peoples of Greenland, Labrador, the Canadian Arctic and Alaska. In this book, it refers to all peoples who speak related languages of the "Eskimo" family.

Fish weir A dam-like construction built across a stream to trap migrating fish. Arctic peoples built weirs of rocks and speared the fish concentrated behind them.

Flakes The waste material produced by knocking chips of stone from flint tools in order to shape or sharpen them. Large, sharp-edged flakes could be used as cutting tools without further shaping.

Gorge-hook A double-pointed stick of bone or wood, tied in the middle to a cord and placed inside a piece of meat. When the bait is swallowed by a fish or gull, the gorge toggles sideways in the animal's throat.

Hafting Any of a variety of techniques by which the point of a weapon is attached to its shaft, or the blade of a knife or other tool to its handle.

Harpoon A specialized weapon for hunting sea mammals. Its head is attached to a line held by the hunter or tied to a float or drag. The head, detachable from the shaft, holds the struck animal either by barbs or by toggling (turning sideways) in the wound.

Historic period The period of time during which there are written records referring to the inhabitants of an area. In the Arctic, the beginning of this period generally coincides with the first penetration by European explorers. In Labrador, the historic period begins in the sixteenth century, while in some parts of the Central Arctic, it begins in the early twentieth century. The period prior to written records is referred to as the prehistoric period.

Ice-creepers Strips of bone or ivory cut with sharp notches and designed to be worn under the feet to prevent the wearer from slipping on the ice.

Inuit The name given to themselves by people speaking the *inutitut* Eskimo language, derived from the work *inuk* which means "man." In this book, the name refers to the historic and late prehistoric occupants of the arctic regions north of Bering Strait and east across the Canadian Arctic to Greenland and Labrador.

Jigging-hook A weighted fish-hook, to which the fish is attracted by an up-and-down jigging motion on the line rather than by bait.

Kayak A hunting boat used throughout the Eskimo world, covered with skin stretched over a light wooden frame, and completely decked except for a hole to accommodate the single hunter. These boats were used for hunting sea mammals, fishing, setting nets, spearing caribou at water-crossings, and for ferrying people across short stretches of water. The forms of kayaks were quite different in various areas, and each was designed for a specific purpose and specific sea conditions.

Komatik The Inuit name for a long, ladder-like sled, built of two strong runners joined by a series of lashed crossbars. Although small sleds could be manhauled, most were designed for dog traction.

Labret Small, carved plugs of ivory, stone or other material worn as decorations in holes pierced through the lower lip or cheeks. These were worn by Alaskan and Mackenzie Delta Eskimos.

Microblade A small, parallel-sided flake of flint with very sharp edges, struck from a specialized micro-blade core. Large numbers of microblades were made by Arctic Small Tool tradition people, and were probably used as cutting and carving tools.

Radiocarbon dating All organic material (wood, bone, etc.) contains a large amount of carbon. While most of this is stable carbon with an atomic number of 12 (C^{12}), a very small proportion is a radioactive isotope (C^{14}), which decays with a half-life of approximately 5500 years. By measuring the relative proportions of C^{14} and C^{12} in an ancient piece of organic material, we can approximate the time that has elapsed since the death of the plant or animal from which the material came. This allows us to give approximate dates to archaeological materials found with such samples.

Scraper A tool made from stone or bone, used to remove the flesh and fatty tissue from animal hides in preparing them for use as clothing or as coverings for boats or tents. Some of the flint objects that archaeologists call scrapers may have been used to carve wood or bone.

Shaman A doctor/magician, someone who has an especially close relationship with the spiritual world. The Inuit *angekok* used his spirit helpers to cure or cause illness, to control the weather, and to bring animals to the weapons of hunters. Shamanic practices are similar across the northern world, both in Eurasia and North America, and may have a common origin in Palaeolithic religious thought.

Sideblade A flint tool mounted in the side of a harpoon or lance head, or in a knife, to form a sharp cutting edge. Arctic peoples seem to have derived this technique from Neolithic cultures of Eurasia.

Sled shoe A flat slab of bone or ivory pegged to the bottom of a sled runner to prevent its damage by rocks or rough ice.

Snow knife A large, flat knife made from whale bone or ivory, used to cut the snow blocks used in building snowhouses.

Snow probe A long, narrow rod of whale bone, used to test the nature of the snow when one wishes to build a snowhouse.

Soapstone A soft stone found in scattered quarries across arctic Canada, used by ancient Eskimos to make lamps and cooking pots, and by their modern descendants to make commercial carvings.

Tundra The vegetation of the area north of the tree line, composed of lichens, mosses, sedges, heaths, and other small flowering plants. Vegetation cover is almost continuous in the southern tundra, while on the northern islands only small and scattered patches are found among the rocks and gravel.

Ulu The semicircular "woman's knife" of the historic Inuit, used to cut meat and fish as well as to cut hides for clothing. In prehistoric times, the blade of the ulu was generally made of slate ground to a sharp edge.

Umiak A large, open boat, about 10 metres long, covered with skins over a wooden frame and propelled by paddles. This boat was used historically for hunting whales, and as a freight boat for moving camp or for travelling long distances.

Index